Jim
Ren
There is such a

Enough About You

I think as
Healthy
Narcissin!

Warmest Regards,

Anne
Hennessy

613-5690867

Enough About You

**THE NARCISSIST'S 7-STEP, 1-MINUTE SURVIVAL GUIDE
TO SACRED SPIRITUALITY, A SELF-EMPOWERED CAREER,
AND HIGHLY EFFECTIVE RELATIONSHIPS**

MIMI E. GOTIST

HarperSanFrancisco
A Division of HarperCollins*Publishers*

HarperCollins books may be purchased for educational, business, or sales promotional use. For information please write: Special Markets Department, HarperCollins Publishers Inc., 10 East 53rd Street, New York, NY 10022.

HarperCollins Web site: http://www.harpercollins.com

HarperCollins®, 📖 ®, and HarperSanFrancisco™ are trademarks of HarperCollins Publishers, Inc.

FIRST EDITION—but not the last, if Mimi has anything to say about it.

Designed and illustrated by the very nearly perfect Kris Tobiassen (the only designer certified by NAANAA, the Narcissists' Affiliated Activist Network of American Assertives).

Library of Congress Cataloging-in-Publication Data is available upon request.

ISBN 0–06–055593–9 (pbk.)

03   04   05   06   07   ❖/QUE   10   9   8   7   6   5   4   3   2   1

To me, me, and only Mimi

Contents

Dear Reader,

This book isn't for you. *You* don't divert every conversation back to yourself, or drop references to your achievements like confetti at every party, or regard the world and all the people in it as pawns on your own personal chessboard.

But do you have friends or—I'm guessing here—family members who fit the profile? Yes, you do. And they have friends too. Millions of them. My publisher is banking on that. So, frankly, am I.

While I'm speaking candidly (which, I've noticed, many best-selling memoirists do), I'd like to share with you the true inspiration for *Enough About You*. Reading the best-seller list one day, I was struck (as I often am) by a penetrating insight: self-help is *so* last-millennium. What the world needs now is *self-hype*.

After all, self-love (as we proud narcissists prefer to call it) is what's au courant today—all the rage (so to speak) of therapists' offices, courtrooms, and corporate boardrooms, of exclusive and mundane social gatherings alike. It is the driving force behind the sports, entertainment, fashion, and insider trading industries, as well as too many other fields and venues to mention (but not too many, my publisher and I fervently hope, to sell books to).

I'm certain, dear reader, that your own interactions and relationships remind you daily, as mine do, that becoming a "better" person is out. Becoming a "stronger" person is in. You could say that narcissism is the *One Minute Manager* of the 2000s; the *Path with Heart* (balls and ovaries actually) of the new millennium, the *Worst-Case Scenario Survival Handbook* for those whose worst-case scenario is endured on a daily, if not hourly, basis: the insensitivity of those around us, who fail to recognize us for exactly whom and what we are.

More than a fad, more than today's trendiest diagnosis, narcissism isn't just for rich people anymore. Narcissologists observe that narcissism is "trickling down," promising to saturate the culture as a whole. I say, the experts are right. And I say, let's give (or better yet, sell) the people what they want.

What they want—what all those narcissists in your life *need*—is *Enough About You*. And think about it: How will they get it *if you don't give it to them?* Only in these pages can narcissists, and people like you who have the great good fortune to care for them, get:

- Practical tips to help narcissists help others (and the whole world, in fact) to conform to our exacting standards.

- True-life anecdotes validating that narcissists, although incredibly special, are not alone.

- An astute critique of the national epidemic of self-doubt, and a clear presentation of the superior model of self-confidence, as embodied by the Superior Self-Lover.

Moving beyond the been-there-done-that era of self-help, *Enough About You* crosses the brave new frontier of self-hype, offering not only the first and only "Me-Q Quiz"—with which narcissists and aspiring narcissists can test their Me-Quotient—but practical, killer-app advice on such hot topics as:

- *Dating:* You're not just looking for the person you want to marry—you're looking for the person you want to change.

- *Sex:* Abstinence makes the fond grow harder.

- *Marriage:* Commit calculated acts of "kindness" and sensible acts of nudity.

- *Career:* Do what makes money and if the love follows, better yet.

- *Spirituality:* Me here now.

- *Personal growth:* You can't help anyone who won't help you.

Enough About You isn't *for* you, dear reader, but it speaks *to* people like you: sophisticated, altruistic, willing and able to drop $11.95 to give the narcissists in your life a gift they truly deserve. No mindless *Narcissism for Dummies, Enough About You* speaks to you as the intelligent, generous, and suggestible-at-the-cash-register human being you know yourself to be.

On a personal note: since I began this project, many people in my life have suggested that no one is better suited to write this book than I. And although their (justifiable) envy casts a cloud of suspicion on their motivations, I must acknowledge that as soon as I sat down to write it, I realized that just this once, my "friends" were right. Just as you were put on earth to buy this book, I was put on this earth to write it.

But enough about me.

When are *you* going to buy my book?

Mine,

Mimi E. Gotist

May 2003
From various Ritz-Carltons
(thanks to you and millions of readers like you)

What's Your Me-Quotient?

Are you a Novice Narcissist, an Intermediate Egotist, or a Superior Self-Lover? Rate your "Me-Q" with this simple seven-step quiz and find out.

Step One: Spirituality

1. You don't deserve this: your girlfriend got a girlfriend, your boss keeps leaving the want ads on your desk, and your pedicurist moved to an ashram in India. For solace, you turn to:

    a. Perspiration (your Spinning class is much like your life: going nowhere fast)

    b. Meditation

    c. Club Med vacation

2. Everyone who's anyone has done the five-day silent retreat at that hot new Zen/Sufi/Vipassana Sacred Healing Center in Sedona. You'd rather go five days without a low-fat triple-shot decaf latte than five days without talking—but your reputation is at stake. You:

a. Go. Bring a tape recorder, so *someone* will be listening when you talk to yourself in the privacy of your own geodesic straw-bale teepee each night.

b. Go. Bring a note from your acupuncturist explaining that you're medically required to take frequent bathroom breaks. Wave off your fellow supplicants' sympathetic looks each time you return from the bathroom (where you've been talking to yourself in the mirror).

c. Don't go. Modestly mention that you've committed to a five-*week* silent retreat (a tour of European art museums actually, but those places are so terribly quiet, and just as boring as meditation).

Step Two: Sex

3. You've rented an erotic film for your evening's entertainment. As you're fast-forwarding past the 900# ads, you hear your ex-lover's voice on your answering machine, begging to see you tonight. You decide to:

a. Ignore the call. You have better things to do. Hit "Play."

b. Pick up the phone. Inform him/her haughtily that you have better things to do. Hit "Play."

c. Pick up the phone. Tell him/her that you had a last-minute cancellation and you'll be over in an hour. (On your way there you'll stop at the video store and insist on a full refund.)

4. Your lover offers you a very special birthday gift: a *ménage à trois* with the third party of your choice. You:

> a. Accept. Ask graciously what your lover will be doing that night.
>
> b. Accept. Ask your lover to invite your best friend. Note response. Dispense punishment accordingly.
>
> c. Decline. Offended by such limited imagination, you arrange for a *real* orgy, to which your lover can only *beg* to be invited.

Step Three: Marriage

5. There's something square and sparkly at the bottom of your flute of Veuve Clicquot, and your lover has an expectant look on his/her face. Marriage? For *you? Jamais!* You:

> a. Chug the champagne. Swallow the ring. Gag, choke, leave. Once you've expelled the ring at home, you can decide whether to (1) keep it; (2) sell it on eBay; or (3) have it melted down into earrings.
>
> b. Ignore the ring. Tell your lover you have one of your "headaches." Take one last medicinal sip (you would *never* waste good champagne!), then go somewhere quiet—your other lover's apartment perhaps—to think the proposal over.
>
> c. "Delightedly" allow your lover to slip the ring onto your finger. Set your internal timer. In five short years, you'll be living on alimony.

6. Your spouse confronts you with incontrovertible evidence of your adultery, demanding either counseling or divorce. You choose:

> a. Counseling. It'll guarantee you one night a week— or more, if you play your cards right—away from the kids.
>
> b. Counseling. Prepared for this eventuality, you've already rehearsed your ever-since-my-father-left-home-when-I-was-30-I've-had-intimacy-issues speech.
>
> c. Divorce. Prepared for this eventuality, you've already had your lawyer draw up the settlement.
>
> **ADD TWO BONUS POINTS for convincing your spouse to sign on the spot.**

Step Four: Parenting

7. Despite your generous "gifts" to the admissions director, your three-year-old has been wait-listed at the best nursery school in town. How will you tell the world?

> a. "Whitney's personal Gymboree trainer tells me that bilingual home-schooling is best for gifted boys like him. We've hired a home-schooling nanny. She's from Paris."
>
> b. "Of course Whitney was accepted. But to best prepare him for a career in the global economy, we've decided to give him a less elite, more diverse academic experience."
>
> c. "We're moving out of state."

8. At nine years old, your daughter never stops whining, and her favorite word is still "mine." You know exactly where this kind of attitude can lead, so you:

   a. Fire the staff. The nanny, the pediatric Rolfer, even the cook have got to go. Where else could your daughter have picked up such unattractive behavior?

   b. Move to a bigger home. If she's going to keep behaving that way, there simply isn't room for the two of you in a four-bedroom, three-bath "starter home."

   c. Try tough love. Take away her American Express card.

Step Five: Career

9. Thanks to your expert mentorship, your personal assistant has just become your boss. You feel:

   a. Thrilled for her. (That's your story, and you're sticking to it—at least until you find another job.)

   b. Stunned by your own competence. Who else could have transformed such a going-nowhere nobody into management material?

   c. Suicidal. You've long believed that there's no justice in this world, and this is final proof.

10. Citing the economic downturn, your company revokes the employee health club benefit. Your response is to:

   a. Quit. They can't do without you; they're sure to offer you a raise and promotion if you'll just change your mind.

b. Secretly organize an employee revolt. Sign someone else's name to the petition. Call in sick the day of the picket line. Return to work, your relationship with management untarnished, when the gym benefit is restored.

c. Be a role model of Buddhist detachment. (It should be easy: you've finally got an excuse not to go to the gym.)

Step Six: Health and Fitness

11. You are simply not a person who gets—*ugh*—pimples. Therefore, the eruption on your chin must be:

a. Ebola. Why must the good die young?

b. Spa malpractice. You didn't have the awful thing *before* you got that apricot/gravel-pit facial yesterday. Luckily, your attorney is on retainer.

c. Your fifth chakra's way of telling you that eating two pints of Chocolate Fudge Brownie Ben & Jerry's in one night is not beneficial to your sacred temple.

12. You've been on the Weight Watchers *and* the Slim-Fast diets *forever* it seems, and you haven't lost an ounce. You:

a. Sue both companies. Corporations must be held accountable for their deceptive advertising.

b. Hire a personal dieting trainer.

c. Resolve to diet for a second day, then reevaluate.

Step Seven: Personal Growth

13. Your therapist says she doesn't feel your work together is productive, so she's terminating your relationship. She hopes that this will be a "useful personal growth experience" for you. You hope that she:

    a. Gains fifteen pounds overnight with no plausible explanation.

    b. Reconsiders. Toward that end, you offer her ten dollars more per "hour" and promise to stop bringing your own couch to your sessions (hers is so *ratty*).

    c. Comes to *you* for help someday, so *she* can benefit from a comparable "personal growth experience."

14. Your Pilates teacher invites you along on a vision quest. When you tell her you're having your aura read that weekend, she pointedly repeats her invitation. You:

    a. Decline firmly. Promise to have your contact lens prescription checked instead.

    b. Accept. On the scheduled day of departure, call to cancel. Explain that you're still in a "visioning process" evoked by the Ecstasy you took the night before.

    c. Accept, on the condition that the quest take place at the Canyon Ranch Spa.

Scoring

1. a–1	b–0	c–2	6. a–1	b–0	c–2	11. a–2	b–1	c–0
2. a–0	b–1	c–2	7. a–0	b–1	c–2	12. a–2	b–0	c–1
3. a–0	b–2	c–1	8. a–2	b–1	c–0	13. a–1	b–0	c–2
4. a–1	b–0	c–2	9. a–0	b–2	c–1	14. a–2	b–1	c–0
5. a–2	b–0	c–1	10. a–1	b–2	c–0			

Twenty Points or More:

SUPERIOR SELF-LOVER Congratulations, you self-adoring specimen, you! You've got your ego right where it belongs: front and center. So when "friends" call you "self-centered," smile proudly and take it as the compliment it is. Whom or what else would you want to be centered on? "In today's confidence-phobic world, self-involvement is often miscast as a *negative* trait," says Shelia Eisenmeese-McCarthy, Ph.D., a clinical psychologist at New York City's Vaine-Frittering Institute. "What a mixed message our culture sends! We are at once advised to love ourselves as we wish to be loved by another, and criticized for loving ourselves too much." But you, "Bright-I's," transcend this cultural chatter, focusing exclusively on that first and foremost loved one: you.

Ten to Nineteen Points:

INTERMEDIATE EGOTIST It takes time and effort to become a Superior Self-Lover, and you, Narcissist-in-the-Middle, are nearly halfway there. Despite an occasional dip into the OP (Ordinary Person) pool, most, if not all, of your choices are satisfyingly self-promotional. "For reasons we don't yet fully understand, some people take to narcissism like a fish without a bicycle," Dr. Eisenmeese-McCarthy says. "Many of these 'Natural Narcissists' have the advantage of being born to narcissist parents. Not everyone can be so fortunate." What's important for *every* aspiring Superior Self-Lover to know is that with an extra soupçon of effort—even absent a positive family history—you too can reach the heights of narcissism easily summited by those "to the manner born."

Nine Points or Less:

NOVICE NARCISSIST Sad but true: you've got your thumb out on the Self-Love Highway, watching the accomplished narcissists zoom by in their Audi TTs. But don't despair. Dr. Eisenmeese-McCarthy says there's hope, even for you. "Besides serving as a useful gauge by which Superior Self-Lovers can measure their success," she counsels, "Novice Narcissists can take pride in knowing that their few achievements result from their own diligent efforts, rather than inherited wealth." Keep striving, Newbie Narci, and remember that by making yourself useful to the Superior Self-Lovers you encounter—shining their shoes, polishing their résumés, perhaps cleaning the occasional window—you can bask, even if just for a moment, in their reflected glory.

Spirituality

Alphabet Soup for the Soul:
The Only Letter That Counts Is "I"

Narcissists don't take well to religion. It clashes with our essential nature; it violates our historic legacy. When Narcissus went looking for love, did he search the skies for some intangible "God" who would never touch or talk to him, tell him how flattering his new haircut was, invite him over for an organic free-range chicken dinner? No, he did not. Narcissus knew whom he could count on: that handsome guy in the pond.

True to our namesake, we narcissists are self-sufficient, self-actualized folk. We have to be: no one ever does enough for us. (Even when they try, they do it so *badly*.) Still, we dream. We keep hope alive. We tell ourselves that the disappointments we endure, the insensitive people with whom we are forced to contend, will make us even stronger than we already are. We tell ourselves that right now, somewhere out there, our special someone is taking an Active Listening seminar, accumulating transferable frequent flyer miles, perhaps purchasing a modest beach home, waiting to give us the nurturing, adoration, and lifestyle that we deserve.

Until we find that special someone, God may have to do.

Whether you call your deity Jesus, Buddha, Allah, Gaia, Shiva, or the confident yet unassuming "Me," even a narcissist needs something to believe in. Something bigger than ourselves—well, maybe not bigger, but *older*. Something outside of ourselves (should we ever choose to go there). Something, certainly, to blame for the worst kind of bad thing that can happen: the kind of bad thing your lawyer can't help you with.

No one—not AAA, not AA, not maps.yahoo.com, not even this book—can give you a road map for your spiritual path. But if you're willing to ask for (and follow) these directions, you may avoid the potholes that all too often rattle narcissists as we travel the road to enlightenment.

Challenge 1: The Notion of Losing Oneself in Prayer

Variously described as "turning it over to God," "catching the spirit," or "becoming one with everything," this spiritual aspiration is anathema to the narcissist. Why would we want to *lose* what we've worked so hard to perfect?

Furthermore, once one loses oneself in prayer, it's just a hop, skip, and a jump down a slippery slope to losing oneself in the religious institution itself.

This challenge presents grave boundary issues for the well-individuated narcissist. In egalitarian religions (such as many Buddhist, pagan, and New Age sects), the supplicant is expected to "blend in with the crowd"—a concept as alien to the narcissist as, say, "doing unto others as you would have them do unto you." In traditional, hierarchical religions, the obvious place for the narcissist is at the top. But what busy narcissist has time to become pope? And why, indeed, should we make the time, given the distressingly delayed return on any spiritual investment?

It is the lonesome burden of narcissists to find ways to stand out in the flock as the special people we are, and receive the recognition we're due—while fiercely guarding our ego strength, time, and money.

You're sitting in the zendo on your zafu, hands clasped in the mudra, legs folded in situ, silently reciting your mantra. "*Om.* I am a speck in the universe . . . an exceptionally beautiful, brilliant, important speck in the universe, but a speck in the universe nonetheless." After a few unproductive minutes, your mind—that precision instrument, so ill suited to emptiness—fills with forbidden thoughts. *Om* . . . becomes *um* . . . then, *I'm*. "I'm . . . probably missing a business call." "I'm . . . sure an hour must have passed by now." "I'm . . . too important to be sitting here doing nothing." Surreptitiously, you check your watch. Three minutes into the hour, you realize that you cannot—indeed, *must* not—continue. Your time is precious. Your enlightenment is at hand. Your foot is asleep.

HOW TO MEET THE CHALLENGE

1. Worship Alone

True, you won't earn the social points that are your rightful due for time spent in public prayer (see Challenge 3 below). But you *will* protect your integrity from the boundary-blurring, identity-obliterating experience of being "one of many" in a place of group worship. Also, assuming that someone is actually up there listening, you can access Him/Her more directly from your DSL line at home.

2. Fake It Till You Make It

For those occasions when home prayer won't do—because there's someone at the church, mosque, or zendo you're trying to impress; because your third eye keeps wandering to the blinking light on your answering machine—you can transcend the tedium of group worship by simulating devotion. During periods of silent group prayer:

- Close your eyes.

- Compose a mental memo, presentation, or grocery list.

- Assign one key point, such as a grocery item, to each finger. This will help you recall your thoughts later.

- If circumstances allow (i.e., if you can safely appear to be jotting down reflections on a sermon or lecture), draft your memo, presentation, or list in the margins of your program, Bible, or Koran.

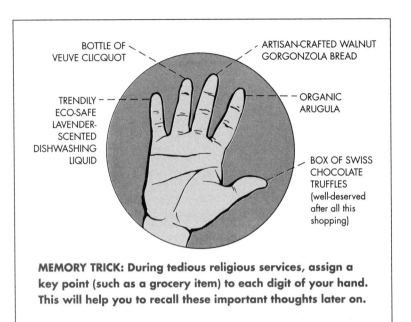

BOTTLE OF
VEUVE CLICQUOT

ARTISAN-CRAFTED WALNUT
GORGONZOLA BREAD

TRENDILY
ECO-SAFE
LAVENDER-
SCENTED
DISHWASHING
LIQUID

ORGANIC
ARUGULA

BOX OF SWISS
CHOCOLATE
TRUFFLES
(well-deserved
after all this
shopping)

MEMORY TRICK: During tedious religious services, assign a key point (such as a grocery item) to each digit of your hand. This will help you to recall these important thoughts later on.

NOTE: The back-lit "Meditation" setting on the *Enough About You*™ Personal Data Organizer allows you to make entries even in the dark without disturbing (or exposing your motives to) your fellow worshipers. It automatically prioritizes appointments and messages as you enter them, based on their ego-gratifying potential. Or, custom-program to sort for career enhancement or other personal goals. $799.95, includes monogrammed reflective titanium case.

WARNING: Imitating prayer may lead to actual spiritual experiences. Do not attempt unless prepared to cope with life-altering consequences.

3. Don't Worship at All

The benefits are clear: time, energy, tithing saved. The downside is less predictable. If the atheists are right, you'll be polishing your résumé, getting your thighs waxed, or writing a new personals ad while others are wasting their time chanting, bowing, and praying. If the atheists are wrong, you might live (or die) to regret your decision. Is there a special place for narcissists—even those who forgo earthly religious affiliation—in the hereafter? Although that seems only fair, in heaven, as on earth, there are no guarantees. Avoid spiritual practice at your own risk.

Challenge 2: The Notion That Spirituality Entails Service to Others

There was a time and a place for distributing loaves and fishes, for leading underprivileged socioeconomic groups across deserts, for fasting to protest occupations by imperialist armies (or cellulite deposits). But that was B.I. (Before Internet). This is now. In the A.I. (After Internet) world, there are many less arduous, more efficient ways to manifest social concerns—genuine or feigned—whether to please an overzealous religious leader, a "socially responsible" boss, or an idealistic but sexy date. With just a few keyboard strokes, we can demonstrate our commitment to our fellow man, woman, or ozone layer by signing a petition, writing to our congressperson, or donating money (if one's accountant deems this tax-beneficial).

The alleged connection between religion and "serving humanity"—one of many quaint but obsolete philosophies prevalent in

Anyone who has davened in a synagogue or made a joyful noise in a church has run into the overly assertive individual we'll call the Divine Do-Gooder. Often operating with the institution's blessing, the DD-G can barely wait until the service is over before s/he starts recruiting congregants to feed the homeless, tutor inner-city children, or march on a picket line. Depending on denomination, the DD-G may present as the spiritual successor of Gandhi, Jesus, or Bella Abzug, using world history, scripture, or the time-honored guilt trip to justify his/her appeals to you to "make a difference," "serve the people," or "leave the world a better place than you found it."

today's mosques, synagogues, churches, and zendos—is the primary cause of an escalating national problem: PTTSA (Pressure To Take Social Action).

HOW TO MEET THE CHALLENGE

1. Just Say No

Whatever anyone says, we narcissists know what spirituality is for: to make us feel better. How can we help others when we're still unenlightened (or overbooked, or taking a beating in the stock market) ourselves? Stand up (or kneel, bow, or squat) and be counted in defense of the principles narcissists hold dear: separation of church and state of mind, the sanctity of a narcissist's right to choose. If you succeed in silencing the DD-G, that will be your contribution to a better world. Handle it in true narcissist style, and you might even convince her/him that *yours* is the more spiritually evolved position.

For your convenience (or in case you're not speaking to your "friends" right now), we rate a small sampling of denominations here.

Christianity ☠

Generally PTTSA-safe, with two crucial exceptions. African American Baptist churches are notorious for confusing prayer with protest, ministering with marching. Until these churches move beyond their unfortunate teach-slaves-to-read–voter registration–Martin Luther King legacy, narcissists are advised to stay away. Equally dangerous are fundamentalist Christian churches, where DD-Gs urge congregants to engage in vociferous, sometimes violent defense of guns, embryos, and "family values."

Buddhism ☠ ☠

Although joining (or purporting to join) any meditation-based religion may be today's most beneficial career and/or dating strategy, many Buddhist faiths also expose you to high doses of PTTSA. Some are affiliated with flagrantly activist organizations, such as the Buddhist Peace Fellowship in (where else?) Berkeley, California. Investigate thoroughly (and check socks) before removing shoes.

Judaism ☠ ☠ ☠

No narcissist can win with this one, particularly considering the insignificant-to-negative career and dating impact of a Jewish affiliation (see Challenge 3 below). If the rabbi isn't exhorting you to send your money or your sons to Israel, it may well be because he (or, for Christ's sake, *she*) is one of those New Age Kaballa types—prime perpetrators of PTTSA. Avoid at all costs.

KEY: ☠ = least risk ☠☠ = moderate risk ☠☠☠ = greatest risk

2. Avoid Socially Conscious Religions

For the most accurate assessment of the PTTSA rating of the religious institutions in your area, we advise you to consult other narcissists, whose places of worship are most likely to be PTTSA-free.

3. Give at the Office

If all else fails, you might try actually making a social contribution on your own, thereby defusing the DD-G's threats that you will damage your karma, burn in hell, or miss the exit for the outlet mall if you don't "give at church."

> **WARNING:** For the Borderline Narcissist, social action may be habit-forming. Do not proceed before checking with your psychotherapist, personal coach, acupuncturist, Pilates teacher, and/or prescribing physician.

Challenge 3: Making Your Spirituality Work for You

Along with the clothes you wear, the car you drive, the school your children attend, and the antidepressants you take, your spiritual affiliation speaks volumes about the position you occupy on the social ladder. In order to maintain your balance on the top rung, you must continually monitor the ever-shifting spiritual landscape, choosing and discarding religions as they become more or less advantageous to your professional, romantic, and physical well-being. (Remember Catholicism? Today you might as well admit to believing in Santa Claus, or the healing power of crystals!)

The operative concept here is nothing less than the principle for which our Founding Fathers fought and died: freedom of religious choice. You're not driving your father's Oldsmobile, are you? If it's not helping you get what you want out of life, you needn't be saddled with his religion either.

HOW TO MEET THE CHALLENGE

You're starting a new job, one you've worked long and hard (okay, manipulated long and hard) to get. During your interviews you took the cultural pulse. You've adjusted your wardrobe, syntax, sexual orientation, and weekend activities accordingly. You're confident that your all-important colleagues—those with the power to hire, fire, and be superseded—will find you comfortably conventional, yet eminently promotable. Just one area of uncertainty remains: you haven't yet been able to ascertain which religious affiliation will contribute most to your success.

1. Do the Research

Discerning the religious predilection of a boss, date, or meter maid requires subtlety and patience—neither, admittedly, an intrinsic forte of the narcissist. The payoff, however—an inside lane on the fast-track to success, a shortcut to the path of least resistance—justifies the investment of time, effort, and (most difficult of all) attention to others. Start with the least strenuous exercises first; escalate as necessary.

- Conduct a surreptitious accessory inspection. Check for crosses, scarabs, Stars of David, ankhs, wedding rings.

- Drop references to the suspect religion (e.g., if your date's name is Sarah Goldenstein, it's best not to start by mentioning Elijah Mohammed). *Useful points of reference:* books you've "read," retreats you've "attended," holidays you've "celebrated," donations you've "made."

- Invite your boss, date, or meter maid to lunch. Allow her to choose the restaurant. Observe what she orders. Order a martini, shellfish, pork, meat loaf, and ice cream for yourself. Offer to share. Observe response.

ADVANCED EXERCISE: If these efforts fail to yield definitive information, take a bite of food from her plate. If she doesn't look horrified, there's an excellent chance that she's Jewish.

2. If You've Got It, Flaunt It

Once you've identified your most advantageous spiritual strategy, miss no opportunity to show your "superiors" at the office, or your contestants in the dating game, that your religious affiliation gives you a "values-added" edge over your competitors. Remember, in the race to enlightenment, it's not just how fast you get there—it's how many people you pass along the way.

- Buy your boss (or your date) modest yet tasteful gifts on shared religious holidays. Be sure to have your name engraved, monogrammed, or printed on the gift in a place where others can't miss it.

- To enhance the spiritual bonding process, speak in spiritual sound bites—coded, if necessary, to avoid violating workplace policies. For example, when your Baptist boss sneezes, substitute "Bless you" for the more emphatic "Praise Jesus!" When your Buddhist boss enters the room, a simple but heartfelt "Hi!" may be more fitting than a bow.

- Attend the place of worship of the person best placed to promote (or sexually satisfy) you. Arrive early. Sit in the last row. See and be seen.

3. If You Can't Get It, Pretend You Got It

Sometimes it's impossible to adopt the religion that would best serve your self-interest: because you can't ascertain which religion that would be; because that religion is not well suited to your lifestyle (praying to Mecca several times a day, for example, can sidetrack even the most self-focused narcissist); or because you've actually got some spiritual beliefs of your own, and despite your best efforts, your inner Christian, Jew, Buddhist, or Zoroastrian will not bow (or kneel or squat) to the more beneficial affiliation.

Even under these difficult circumstances, a narcissist can accrue "piety points" by broadening the definition of "religious experience" to include such soul-altering events as:

- A stay at a spa.

- A stint in rehab.

- A weekend Rolfing workshop.

- An especially stirring shopping experience.

- Sex with someone you know.

NOTE: Throwing the I Ching takes time, coins, and concentration—after all, it was invented five thousand years ago, when people had that kind of time and money. The limited edition *Enough About You*™ "Me-Ching" is for modern-day narcissists who need affirmation and validation *now*. Just toss the pebble into the cup, watch for your reflection, smile when you see it, and go on about your business. $69.99 includes Zen pebbles, Chinese Heavenly Bamboo cup, and recycled rubber splash guard made from the soles of Mayan peasants' huaraches.

With practice, you'll learn to drop seamless, convincing references to your "transformative retreat" (six days/five nights at the Maui Hilton); your "vision quest" (search for, and purchase of, the very sunglasses worn by Carrie on *Sex in the City*); and your "overnight epiphany" (following discovery of your best friend in bed with your lover).

Sex

The Seventy-Minute Orgasm (Yours)

Even under the most hygienic conditions, sex presents the narcissist with a sticky situation. We know sex is good for us—otherwise, why would we be such avid consumers of products that replicate its effects: cosmetics for postcoital glow, pharmaceuticals for postcoital relaxation, yoga postures for midcoital maneuvers? Occasionally (though not nearly often enough, due to others' inadequacies), sex may actually evoke pleasure—the sensation that is the narcissist's very raison d'être, although, *mon dieu!,* we are deprived of it far too often.

Finally, for advanced narcissists determined to embark on that lifestyle-of-maximum-difficulty—marriage—sex is a troublesome but necessary hump to overcome, so to speak, in the process of identifying, pursuing, and netting a husband, wife, domestic partner, or sugar daddy.

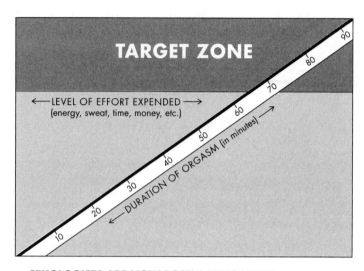

TARGET ZONE

←—LEVEL OF EFFORT EXPENDED —→
(energy, sweat, time, money, etc.)

DURATION OF ORGASM (in minutes) →
10 20 30 40 50 60 70 80 90

**SEXOLOGISTS ARE NOW POSTULATING WHAT
NARCISSISTS HAVE LONG KNOWN:** any orgasm of less
than 70 minutes in duration is simply not worth having.

Superhuman though we seem, narcissists are in fact mortal. When the flesh calls—even if we've set it on "Vibrate"—we too must answer. But rather than trudging resentfully onto the sexual playing field, seeing sex solely as the fraught undertaking that it can admittedly be, narcissists should instead take pride in the special attributes that we alone bring to the fray.

Unlike OPs (Ordinary Persons), narcissists are impervious to the cultural myths—perpetrated by Hollywood movies, romance novels, feminist ideologues, and wedding vows—that render sex even more problematic than it need be. We alone have the self-confidence it takes to reject out of hand (and orifice) such sentimental goals as "soul-merging sex," "mutual orgasm," and "becoming one with each other"—the unattainable aspirations that cause so many sexual encounters between consenting OPs to end with the sad, silent question, "Is that all there is?"

This is a question narcissists need not ask. We know exactly what there is, and what we're in it for: *the largest number of top-quality, seventy-minute (or longer) orgasms received in return for the smallest possible expenditure of energy, time, money, and (ugh) perspiration.*

By keeping the Narcissist's Sexual Credo—also known as the Seventy-Minute Rule—top-of-mind (and/or top-of-relevant-organs), and by following the simple guidelines spelled out in this chapter, narcissists can experience far more productive, possibly even *pleasurable* sexual encounters—the kind that end with the far more upbeat query, "Could you get me a cigarette?"

Challenge 1: *Ménage à Un:* Making Love with That Special Someone

Every narcissist knows the wisdom of the age-old saying, "If you want something done right, and no truly first-class professional is available, do it yourself." Nowhere is that pearl of wisdom more applicable than to the matter of physical self-love. Regarded by the OP as strictly second-best, sex with oneself has far greater potential for the self-starting narcissist, who can readily summon the creativity, self-awareness, and flair that satisfying self-sex requires.

Some sacrifices, nonetheless, must be made. The Novice Narcissist, new to the joys of self-adoration, may long for the thrill—however fleeting and superficial—of being adored by another. Even the Superior Self-Lover may feel a bit triste, experiencing *la petite mort* without an audience of at least one. After all, what self-respecting narcissist wants to die even a little death alone, without an impressive, well-dressed turnout?

It's Saturday night, and somehow the unthinkable has come to pass. You have no date, no prospects, and—more incredibly still—*Law and Order* isn't on, even in reruns. Your sexual clock is ticking; it's been *days* since your body has had the kind of attention it needs to support the well-oiled machine that is your life.

Your options are limited: sublimation (with or without the help of your usual stand-ins, Ben & Jerry), humiliation (will that three-boyfriends-ago ex-boyfriend *really* be glad to hear from you tonight?), or masturbation.

The narcissist's top priority—to eschew the twin evils of cellulite and indignity at all costs—dictates your choice. So you begin. You engage in some light but stimulating foreplay. (When the afterglow fades, Windex will remove the lipstick kisses from the mirror.) You turn up the volume on the answering machine (ever receptive to a better offer). And then you gather your battery-operated accoutrements, your pleasures, and your rosebuds where you may.

HOW TO MEET THE CHALLENGE

1. Seduce Yourself

For the narcissist, there's no such thing as "playing" hard to get. We *are* hard to get, and well worth the effort of the chase. So, woo yourself with all the passion and finesse you'd demand of any suitor. Insist on buying yourself dinner; impress yourself by getting last-minute reservations at the hottest spot in town. Order champagne; revel in your company. Over appetizers, compliment your hair, your clothes, your scintillating repartee. Take your hand as you're waiting for the valet; steal a few caresses in the car. Once you've been invited in, it's time to set the scene.

- Light candles—dozens of them. (Whatever the rosemary-pumice facial wrap missed, the flickering light will conceal.)

- Softly play the CD of mood music you've burned for the occasion: "Nobody Does It Better," followed perhaps by "You're the One That I Want."

- Uncork a bottle of your favorite wine. Notice how attentive you are to your every like and dislike—a portent of sensual pleasures to come.

- When you just can't wait another moment, use every word in your body language to say, "I want you. I need you. And I won't take no for an answer."

- Seventy minutes (or more) later, as the bonfire of your passion cools to glowing embers, *resist the urge to fall asleep.* Remember, this is more than a one-night fling. Murmur words of praise and gratitude, promises of undying love.

2. Don't Fake Your Orgasm

As crucial as it is for narcissists to maintain our prestige in the eyes of others, it's even more imperative that we think highly of ourselves. No narcissist wants to believe that he or she is any less than the sexiest, most responsive, most highly orgasmic creature on

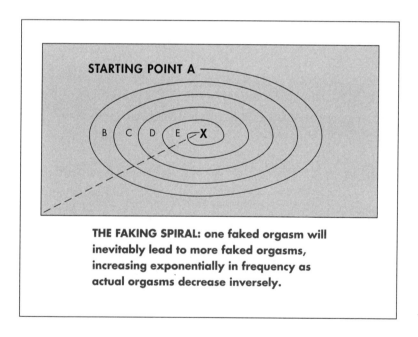

THE FAKING SPIRAL: one faked orgasm will inevitably lead to more faked orgasms, increasing exponentially in frequency as actual orgasms decrease inversely.

earth. Failing (oh! that awful word!) to reach a climax during self-sex can be just as demoralizing, if not more so, than leaving a two-way sexual encounter with one's rocks not yet off.

But remember: you are the most sensitive, forgiving, motivated lover you will ever have. A frightening thought, perhaps, but true. If you fake orgasm once—especially if your deception is successful—you'll be tempted to take the easy way out (and off) again and again. Be honest. Be assertive about what you need. And hope against hope that your words will fall on compassionate ears.

3. Love the One You're With

Rather than seeing self-sex as the second-best choice (it can't be, or no narcissist would choose it), learn to see it as the best choice there is. Relish the plethora of sexual benefits to be reaped when your lovemaking relies on "Nobody But You."

- You're having sex with the only person who truly loves you, the only person you truly love. In self-sex you realize the impossible dream: security and passion in the same sexual encounter.

- You won't be bothered by the annoying demands that partners all too often make—whether emotional (see "sentimental goals" above) or logistical ("Do we *always* have to do it in front of a mirror?").

- Loving only you, you're free to engage in sexual escapades that might daunt a lesser partner: nontraditional positions (limited, of course, to those that allow you to remain flatteringly arranged in the mirror) and other erotic adventures.

NOTE: Executing the dominatrix role during solo sex may be both physically challenging and uneconomical. The *Enough About You*™ Wrist Restraint, $69.99, is the only brand sold in sets of one.

Challenge 2: *Ménage à Deux*

There are two possible scenarios for sex with another person. One is ideal for the narcissist; the other is anything but.

The former is the one-night stand (also known as "the audition"). In this encounter the narcissist's gifts shine brightly as in no

---

You meet at a party. The decision to leave together is mutual, immediate, and unexpectedly satisfying: Who knew how valid the correlation between foot size and bed-linen thread count would prove to be?

Forgoing afterglow, you rise gracefully from the tangled yet butter-soft sheets, gather your clothes from the floor, curtain rods, kitchen countertops. You return to the bedroom for a quick farewell kiss, a fitting end to an encounter you've already filed under "Slam, bam, tell me how great I am."

But your bedmate has other plans. S/he pulls you into a suffocating embrace. "Can't you stay the night?" s/he whines.

You've been here before. You know where this is going. It would be cruel to delay the inevitable. You remove your tongue from your lover's mouth, your Grey Goose from his/her freezer, your oatmeal-chamomile soap from his/her bathroom, and let yourself out.

other. The narcissist's forte, after all, is the first impression. (What with people projecting their flaws onto us as they do, things tend to get dicey after that.)

> **WARNING:** As appealing as the one-night stand may be, there *is* risk involved. Some encounters, masquerading as the genuine item, may actually be Gateway Schtups that open the door to more treacherous situations. See "relationships" below.

Gateway Schtups, in which sex persists for longer than one night, may put the narcissist on a collision course with his or her worst-case scenario: a relationship. The list of unpleasantries associated with this outcome is longer than a narcissist's letter to Santa, and should be avoided at all costs.

HOW TO MEET THE CHALLENGE

1. *Ménage à Trois* . . . or More

Many of the problems arising from sex between two people have a simple mathematical solution: add one (or more). Once you've augmented the cast of characters, and your understudy (or understudies) has disposed of any errant sexual needs that might otherwise mistakenly be directed at you, you can lie back and enjoy your starring role in the show. Just be sure that the menagerie understands the terms of the ménage: you, your partner, and any invited guests are all there in service of the same greater goal—to give you *the largest number of top-quality, seventy-minute orgasms received in return for the smallest possible expenditure of energy, time, money, and (ugh) perspiration.*

NOTE: The Narcissist's Sexual Credo is spelled out in tin letters, hand-hammered by Oaxacan craftspersons, on the *Enough About You*™ Wall Plaque, $39.99. Perfect for display in your bedroom or home office, the plaque is crafted from redolent redwood recycled from Provençal wine barrels. Or, proclaim your narcissist pride at your own front door, with the *Enough About You*™ Doormat, woven from hand-spun Tahitian sisal. Buy one, don't be one. $29.99.

2. Go Mute

There are many unmistakable warning signs that a fling is headed down a slippery slope; only a small sampling is represented here.

- You're artfully arranged in bed, waiting for your lover to minister to your every desire. S/he says s/he wants to "talk first."

- The word "issues" has replaced the word "hot" in her/his vocabulary.

- The passionate lover who once whisked you away for sexy spa weekends now "surprises you" with a standing appointment for couples counseling every Tuesday night.

These problems, and others too numerous to list, can all be solved by eliminating one onerous interaction: the two-way conversation. In eras past, the graceful yet final "I don't want to talk about it" would have sufficed. But in today's postfeminist world, successfully avoiding conversation requires a more creative approach.

When your body is fully sated, your goal (mounted above your bed, the *Enough About You*™ Wall Plaque serves as a handy reminder) accomplished:

■ Turn to your partner. Croak something unintelligible.

■ Scribble a note explaining that you suffer from PCL (Post-Coital Laryngitis) and must recuperate at home, alone.

■ Accept your lover's sympathies. Leave.

■ Repeat after the next tryst. And the next.

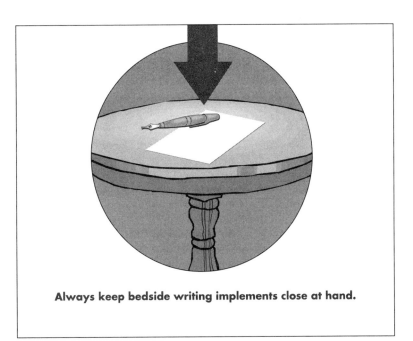

Always keep bedside writing implements close at hand.

If your lover persists in pressing for conversation, thereby proving too self-absorbed to support you in your recovery, see option 3 below.

3. Just Say Go

Once you've bent over backward (and/or forward and sideways, in every room of the house) to meet your lover's needs, but s/he remains insatiable—insisting that you "reciprocate," pleading for praise under the guise of asking "how it was for you"—you have no choice but to bid her/him *adieu*. For the Novice Narcissist, still subject to vestigial pangs of empathy, it may help to focus on the fact that *your lover's own flaws*—self-centeredness, fear of intimacy, inability to nurture—*triggered his/her devastating loss.* Perhaps your soon-to-be-ex will learn from this experience; perhaps not. That is not your concern. Remember: you can't help anyone who won't help you.

Challenge 3: *Ménage à Rien*

Never a lifestyle even an Ordinary Person would choose, abstinence is to narcissists what Kryptonite is to Superman, what scissors are to paper, what a grand jury is to Martha Stewart. Righteously secure though we may be, even the most confident narcissist can hear his/her death knell tolling—"Loser, loser," it cries—when forced to endure hours, days, *weeks* without sex. And no wonder: abstinence, and the self-doubt that it engenders, is nothing short of life-threatening to the narcissist. How can we be expected to go a week without sex, when we can't go a day without applause?

Narcissists are not victims. We are not people to whom "life happens." We are people who happen to life. Still, there are circumstances that even we cannot "overcome": a temporary but unsavory genital condition; the untenable combination of a roommate, a noisy toy or lover, and a thin bedroom wall; the pernicious presence of a pimple of Vesuvian dimensions.

To "overcome" these hurdles we must rise to the challenge, dig deep into the narcissist's repertoire, and make like a Maytag: *spin, spin, spin.* The accomplished narcissist will convince not only him/herself but others that abstinence is neither a scourge visited upon him or her, nor a mere choice. It is, rather, an *aspiration achieved.*

It's been weeks, and you've learned all too well the truth of the cliché. Abstinence makes the fond grow harder—and the waistline thicker and the mood dourer. Doing without, you find it challenging to function at the unparalleled level that you—indeed, the world—have come to expect and demand.

But even as the blood slows to sludge in your veins, even as you wake, day after day, from tormented dreams of Havana cigars, erupting volcanoes, the Washington Monument, your sense of self-worth prevails. You look beyond immediate gratification to visualize a brighter tomorrow: you see yourself in your rightful place atop the sexual heap, having the best sex, early and often, with the most enviable partners. Until the day your fantasy, and you yourself, come to fruition, you keep your upper lip (and only your upper lip) stiff, your imagination (and only your imagination) fertile, and yourself (remember, it's temporary) firmly in hand.

HOW TO MEET THE CHALLENGE

1. Take Pride in Your Discretion

Ordinary Persons are celibate for one reason, and one reason alone: they can't find anyone willing to have sex with them. Celibate narcissists are motivated by precisely the opposite phenomenon: we can't find anyone *worthy* of having sex with us.

When one's ego strength is undermined by celibacy's erosive effects, even the lifelong narcissist may become susceptible to doubts normally experienced only by the OP—for example, the feeling that you are the one being rejected, not the one doing the rejecting. Should these misconceptions arise, it's crucial to interrupt them before they cause psychological damage that could cost the price of a Jag S-Type to heal.

> **ADVANCED EXERCISE:** List the come-ons you turn down daily: the construction worker who begged for just one kiss; your best friend's wife who swears at every party that it's you she truly wants; the teenage delivery boy whose hand brushed yours, oh so deliberately, as you took possession of your tandoori. Tally up the evidence that your options are in fact abundant; give yourself discretionary credit where credit is due.

2. If You Can't Get What You Want, Reframe What You've Got

Abstinence is in the eye—and the sound bite—of the beholder. Although even narcissists are not always able to control the breadth of our sexual opportunities, we *can* control the way others perceive it.

Should "friends" comment upon your celibate lifestyle, remind them: it's not that you're not getting any. It's that you're not *accepting* any.

don't say

"I feel like I'm staggering through a sexual Sahara, dying of thirst, with no end (or even a nice set of pecs) in sight."

do say

"I'm engaged in a new and incredibly energizing spiritual practice called sexual abstention."

don't say

"I'm so jealous of all that sex you're having, I could die."

do say

"Someday, maybe *you'll* be evolved enough to practice sexual abstention too."

don't say

"I could go a month without shaving and no one would even *notice.*"

do say

"I can't believe all the money I'm saving, not having to wax all the time."

don't say

"I'm so horny I gave my phone number to a fire hydrant today."

do say

"I finally finished *Finnegan's Wake.*"

ADVANCED EXERCISE: Advertise to teach a course called "Abstinence as a Path to Enlightenment." Screen your "student body" judiciously. Identify one (or more) of your applicants who can render you unqualified to teach the course. Cancel the course. Matriculate.

3. Lie

Once you've become expert at silently visualizing your ideal sexual scenario, it's only a hop, skip, and a hump to "visualizing" it aloud, in public, glowingly, and in vivid detail. Unlike most people, when you talk about your "dream lover," you'll be speaking literally. And if your "visualization" proves convincing, start taking notes and interviewing agents. The publishing world is still looking for the next *Bridget Jones's Diary.*

Marriage

I Did, I Do, Now Do I Have To?: Narcissists Need Love Too

Marriage, simply put, is about sharing. Narcissists, simply put, are not. Narcissists are about diversity of experience (sometimes referred to by lesser beings as "promiscuity"), self-actualization (often misconstrued as "opportunism"), and independence (commonly misinterpreted as "selfishness"). Marriage celebrates none of these attributes.

Yet against all odds, narcissists do marry. Some, incredibly, stay that way. Others bravely attempt this challenging exercise not once, but repeatedly. Despite the intrinsic incompatibility between the narcissist and this lifestyle (or "dead-style," as it is known to many who have endured it), the incentives to pursue it are significant as well.

The precocious or mature narcissist may have grown weary of suffering life's daily indignities uncosseted by the soothing effect of a loving spouse waiting at home to rub his feet; cook her a nice, hearty, yet low-fat Pacific Rim or perhaps fusion dinner; review all available cellphone plans and wait on hold to secure the best one. Having been around the relationship block a few times (see Step Two: Sex, Challenge 2: *Ménage à Deux*), the experienced narcissist may realize the wisdom of snatching up, so to speak, the rare lover with the staying power to sustain the level of care that the narcissist needs and deserves—bad hair day after missed promotion day, PMS after PMS, quarter-life crisis after midlife crisis, year after year.

The ambitious narcissist, ever-alert to all-important image considerations, may choose marriage for the career-enhancing move that it is. Feminist rhetoric notwithstanding, the narcissist professional (not to be confused with the professional narcissist) knows that singlehood is acceptable *only* up to age twenty-nine for females and age forty-nine for males, and becomes a career impediment after that. The narcissist with a keen eye toward the future may marry for the retirement benefits ("alimony") and/or the postmatrimonial conversion value of the material goods (2.5-carat diamond ring, jewel-encrusted Rolex) accrued during the marriage.

Finally, narcissists marry because we need a backup plan for the one, two, sometimes *four weeks at a time* when our therapists—manifesting callous disregard for the object constancy that they, above all others, know that we need—go on vacation.

Challenge 1: The Tyranny of Sharing

Where did the notion come from that marriage must entail sharing? Kindergarten? Jonathan Livingston Seagull? Marla Maples Trump? Certainly Oprah Winfrey must take her share of the blame. Whatever its origin, this outmoded, oppressive paradigm persists.

Sharing may be well suited to the Ordinary Person, whose boundaries are blurry if they exist at all, whose sense of purpose is hopelessly intertwined with that of others, who stands to *gain* by merging with a mate. But expecting a self-directed, well-individuated narcissist to live his or her life to the fullest while simultaneously

It's your night to cook, and you've decided to go all out (all take-out—but you picked it up yourself). Your spouse comes home, grabs a microbrew from the fridge. Oblivious to the candles you've thoughtfully lit, the chopsticks you've laboriously removed from their wrappers, the Mu Shu you've meticulously transferred from cardboard carton to hand-painted platter, s/he launches into an excruciatingly boring story about . . . something. You lose interest before the Evian has been poured.

Above the endless narrative, your marriage counselor's instructions ring in your ears. So you try—really try—to "give your spouse the kind of attention you expect in return." But the voice of justice rises from deep within. "Shut up already!" it shouts. Your spouse looks mortified. Apparently you've spoken aloud. "When I talk, it's interesting," you explain patiently. "When you talk, it's not."

sharing it with another—this is the moral and practical equivalent of clamping a Denver boot onto a Porsche, then stepping on the gas.

In its ideal form, marriage is a complementary division of labor, each partner nurturing and building on the other's strengths. And so, in the give-and-take of a long-term relationship, narcissists must leave the giving to those who do it well, focusing our energies instead where they will be most effective, the "taking" side of the equation.

HOW TO MEET THE CHALLENGE

1. Redefine "Active Listening"

Practiced as we are at multitasking—meditating while writing grocery lists (Step One: Spirituality), having orgasms while timing them (Step Two: Sex)—narcissists bring new meaning to the communications tool known as "active listening."

When your spouse initiates conversation, that's your cue to initiate action: a readily concealed project (nail polish–drying, bald spot–massaging, Kegels muscle–flexing) that you can accomplish *while* you're leaning forward in your seat, cocking your head attentively, and nodding at strategic intervals.

2. Tip the Scales

Narcissists are, by nature, masters of self-assessment. We know where our strengths lie; we don't waste time pursuing skills that are (a) unattainable or (b) not worth having. *Case in point:* the quaint but self-effacing phenomenon known as "giving."

To fulfill our role in the delicate *pas de deux* of marriage while retaining our incisive self-focus, narcissists can achieve a convincing

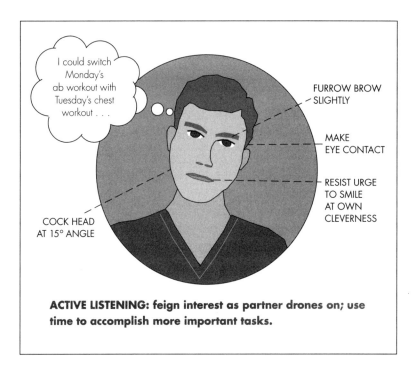

ACTIVE LISTENING: feign interest as partner drones on; use time to accomplish more important tasks.

imitation of giving—and accrue "giving credits"—by *committing calculated acts of "kindness" and sensible acts of nudity.*

■ Get the most bang for your "giving" buck: buy the cheapest gifts from the most expensive stores; have them gift-wrapped; shrug off protestations that once again you've "given too much."

■ Each year, learn six things no one else knows about your spouse: favorite sushi combination platter, sexual fantasy, *Sopranos* season. Note them in your *Enough About You*™

Personal Data Organizer. Every other month surprise your spouse with a gift that "no one else could give." This will silence the spouse who's been hinting that you're not "attentive enough." Amortized over the likely life span of your marriage, this outcome represents an excellent return on investment.

NOTE: The *Enough About You*™ Personal Data Organizer is the only PDA recognized by NAANAA (Narcissists' Affiliated Activist Network of American Assertives).

3. Roll Over and Play Vulnerable

Although the saying "Tis better to give than to receive" does not apply to the narcissist, it might well have been written with the spouse of the narcissist in mind. Give your partner the gift of giving (to you):

- Present your righteous request for attention (sometimes mistaken as "insatiable neediness") as "vulnerability" instead.

- Stop venting your revenge fantasies; start "revealing" your "innermost wounds and fears."

- Instead of complaining about other people's problems, speak touchingly of "your own."

Only the most heartless spouse will dare to issue that tiresome complaint—"Will you *ever* stop *whining?*"—when you're sobbing "helplessly" in his/her arms.

Challenge 2: The Less Things Change, the More They Stay the Same

Narcissists need variety the way foreheads need Botox: we just can't get properly plumped up without it. How can we be at our best if we restrict ourselves to one life partner night after been-there-done-that night? How can we retain our characteristic *joie de moi*, seeing the same face over the breakfast table, hearing the same tired set of compliments, day after redundant day? Like a chef preparing steak tartare, the narcissist needs fresh meat—a constant supply of new excitement about the wonder that is "I."

You accepted the ring (Cartier). You said the vows (Gibran/Dr. Phil). You hyphenated your name (his first, yours last). Six months later the sexual maneuvers, the secret-recipe raspberry vinaigrette, and the adoring glances that first seduced you have become stultifyingly predictable. The amorous suitor who once ripped the bikinis off his "favorite tart" now goes to bed early with briefs and torts.

You're still committed to your life partner (at least until his/her firm makes him/her a partner). But you need so much more. And you know where to get it. There's a new, attractive person at your office (coincidentally, also on partner track) whose admiring eyes follow you wherever you go . . .

HOW TO MEET THE CHALLENGE

1. Push the Envelope

Injecting the new and different into a marriage that's become old and stale is a dirty job. But unless you've married a narcissist—in which case the situation is hopeless (see Challenge 3)—you're the someone who's got to do it. If you value your vows, your commitment, your share of the marital assets, put that famous dramatic flair of yours to work.

- Tell your spouse to meet you in a crowded bar.
- Wear a wig, new clothes, unfamiliar perfume, a seductive smile.
- Hand him/her the key to a hotel room.
- Slip off the bar stool. Go to the hotel room. Wait.
- Observe response.

INTERMEDIATE EXERCISE: If s/he recognizes you and takes the bait, enjoy a night of "like-new" excitement.

ADVANCED EXERCISE: If s/he doesn't recognize you and shows up in the hotel room anyway, enjoy a night of "like-new excitement." Then remove the wig, blow your own cover, and claim the "infidelity credits" you've just earned, redeemable at your own discretion.

NOTE: Whether you're perched on a barstool or plodding on a StairMaster, you can check discreetly for telltale signs of desperation—or perspiration—using the *Enough About You*™ Pocket Mirror. Reflective chrome case, built-in flattering lighting. $22.50 includes blemish-concealer stick.

NOTE: Whether your scene is a suburban singles club, a downtown leather bar, or a transgender drag show, the *Enough About You*™ Fragrance Line—Parfum Pour Les Femmes, Cologne Pour Les Hommes, Eau De Toilette Pour Les Autres—will ensure that you get what you came for. Available in cut-glass Lalique decanter ($250/flacon) or sensible Steuben ($50/soupçon).

2. Get Help

If you enjoy dental work without anesthesia (or insurance), you may choose to engage in marriage counseling: probing your "intimacy issues" and your spouse's, exploring "why neither of you is getting your needs met." Or you can do it the Narcissist's Way—less pain, more gain: hire a small staff of trained professionals who can actually solve the problem. A personal trainer, image consultant, personal shopper, stylist, and colorist (envious "friends" might call them sycophants; you'll know them as your "support team") can supply the attention, admiration, and flattery you're no longer getting at home. If your spouse questions the expense, pointedly explain that you're taking "marital vitamins," supplementing needed nutrients missing from your regular diet.

3. Open Your Marriage (to You)

There are only two ways out of a marriage that's lost its luster: the door marked "Divorce" and the door marked "Other"—lovers, that is. Avoid the tacky muss and fuss of cheating; come clean (so to speak) instead and tell your spouse you want an open marriage.

If s/he responds *too* enthusiastically, quickly explain that you're the one—the only one—to whom the new "open door policy" applies. If you've married well, s/he will eagerly comply, grateful for this chance to keep you despite his/her chronic neglect. If you haven't (telltale indicator: s/he demands equal access), it might be time to try your key in that other door.

Challenge 3: Finding Your Sole Mate

Having chosen to enter the Olympian contest of marriage, the narcissist now faces another, more daunting trial: finding a suitable partner for the match. Surveying the pool of qualified candidates from where the narcissist stands—at the pinnacle of human achievement—we experience profoundly the loneliness at the top.

An Ordinary Person, of course, will not do. Even if our marital motivation is fiduciary, our investment transitory, we simply cannot allow ourselves to sink that low. Marrying one of our own kind is equally inconceivable. Trying to fit two narcissists into one marriage is like trying to fit a size 12 body into a pair of size 8 jeans—guaranteed to cut off the oxygen supply to vital organs, if it's possible at all.

It is the task, then, of the nuptially challenged narcissist to identify the candidate who embodies the best of both: the charisma, charm, good looks, and self-assurance of the narcissist; the affability, flexibility, and selflessness of the OP. Your life partner is the mir-

You've been kissing frogs till you croak; you've baited, lured, and thrown back nearly every fish in the sea. But now you've met someone who has made your heart (and other body parts) stand up and take notice: someone who possesses the pot of gold at the end of every gold-digger's rainbow: that rare, elusive attribute, True Marriage Potential (TMP).

S/he is neither too dull to bear nor too captivating to borrow (as if *anyone* could steal) your thunder in a crowd; affluent enough to keep you in the style to which you're eager to become accustomed, but not enough to threaten your status as power broker in this (and every) dynamic. His/her attractiveness—understated yet undeniable—sets yours off nicely, without provoking untoward comparisons. You're seriously considering taking the next step: learning his/her name. But before you make this commitment, you need to know: Could this be the real thing?

ror that reflects your tastes, your prowess, your status. When you gaze into that mirror, whether once or one thousand times, you've got to like what you—and your boss and others who can influence the course of your life—see.

HOW TO MEET THE CHALLENGE

1. Do a Reference Check

In the workplace hiring process, the protocol is unquestioned: the employer obtains a list of previous bosses, asks probing questions about performance, attitude, and attributes, and makes a decision based upon data received.

Although marriage is often a less permanent relationship, the same due diligence is required. When screening a marital candidate, start by dropping gentle hints ("What did you say your first husband's phone number was?"). If your candidate doesn't willingly offer the necessary information, less forthright methods may be called for:

- "Borrowing" his/her *Enough About You*™ Personal Data Organizer.

- "Running into" his/her exes at the gym, the market, their front doors.

- Interviewing each ex, as you encounter them, about their predecessors.

If your investigation inadvertently goes public, remind your potential spouse how fortunate s/he is to be in the running—and that in this, as in all matters of the heart, mind, and body, the end justifies the meanness.

2. Climb the Family Tree

Although the RH (Relationship History) factor is a crucial element of the prenuptial exploration, family history is critical as well. Early in the relationship (sometime after the first seventy-minute orgasm but well before the first kiss), tenderly ask your candidate to "bring you home to meet Mom." Once you've gained entry to the family domicile, use stealth, wits, and a passing reference to a bladder infection to cover your tracks as you:

- Check all rooms for trophies, awards, and framed photos of your intended. A scarcity is a sure sign of an OP; excessive display could indicate latent narcissism.

- Ascertain the birth order of your candidate. If he's the oldest child, rule him out. If she's the youngest child, rule her out. If he's the middle child, ask how old he was when he opened his first savings account.

- Interview all family-of-origin members. Take notes.

if they	you should
Speak dotingly of your candidate as "the baby of the family"	Call a cab

if they	you should
Speak reverently of your candidate as "the golden boy/girl of the family"	Call a cab

if they	you should
Mention your candidate's "past," then kick each other under the table	Call a cab

if they	you should
Take you on a tour of the tasteful, expensive gifts your intended has bought each of them over the years	Call a jeweler

3. Return for Repairs

Like a tastefully composed Armani ensemble, True Marriage Potential sometimes appears not in black and white but in ambiguous shades of gray. If your candidate shows great potential but also manifests a few troubling flaws, don't despair. Remember, you're not just looking for the person you want to marry—you're looking for the person you want to change.

"Lovingly" suggest that the inability to nurture that hurts you so might also affect his/her relationships with others. Wonder aloud if that "doormat quality" that you find so unattractive might be holding him/her back on the job as well. Mention a few options ("You could get into therapy several times a week, sweetheart, or I could dump you right here and now"), then wait patiently (allow at least two sessions) for desired results.

WARNING: Do not try this at home! Transforming a marital candidate from a "definite maybe" to a "yes" is a time-consuming, often tiresome endeavor best left to professionals who have nothing better to do.

STEP FOUR

Parenting
Raising Clone: There's a Reason They Call It "Reproduction"

The reasons for narcissists to avoid parenting as assiduously as we would avoid any other life-threatening situation are obvious and abundant. Even for those with the resources required to raise one's progeny in a civilized fashion (hiring the job out to trained professionals), child-rearing unavoidably involves much that is anathema to all but the most ordinary of Ordinary Persons. It's demanding (and not in the good, listen-to-me-because-I'm-worth-it way). It's expensive (and not in the good, I-paid-full-price-at-Barney's-and-it-shows way). It's messy (and not in the good, I'm-married-but-I-want-you-anyway way). And it's fattening (there is no good way).

Yes, God made nannies, housekeepers, private schools, and cosmetic surgeons to address troublesome issues such as these. But even with staff support, the return on the childbearing investment falls far from justifying the expense. For a narcissist, being pro-life (pro-*having* a life, that is) is inexorably linked to childlessness.

Why is it, then, that so many narcissists risk all that they have worked so hard to build—impressive careers, white wool-carpeted homes, twenty-six-inch waistlines, bank accounts full of undisposed-of disposable income—to cross the fecundity frontier? Scratch the surface of a Breeder Narcissist who extolls the joys of parenting, and you're likely to find (a) an upwardly married narcissist whose lawyer failed to extricate him/her from a prenup childbearing clause, (b) a middle-management narcissist whose boss has six children and promotes only "family people," or (c) a Novice Narcissist who thinks children are "worth the effort" (and also believes that denial is a river in Egypt).

If any or all of these circumstances apply to you, don't despair. Between the ages of six and eleven,[1] children can make lovely reflective accessories. Like tiny, jewel-encrusted mirrors, their little lives offer proof of your success, good taste, and superior judgment: the schools to which you are able to get them accepted, the stylish clothes in which you are able to dress them, the French phrases that you (the Parisian nanny actually, but who did the hiring?) are able to teach them. Later there will be the prestigious rehab and wilderness programs to which you are able to exile them, and—should you opt to grow old instead of taking the more graceful way out—the adorable grandchildren upon whom you (the latest Parisian nanny actually, but you'll provide the funding) will dote.

---

[1] To cope with children of other ages, even this book will not suffice; consult your team of helping professionals.

Best of all, having a child will put to rest all those jealousy-fueled accusations you've had to endure all your life. Who could be "unbearably self-absorbed" and "ruthlessly ambitious" and be a parent too? What greater humanitarian act could you commit than to bestow upon this earth another person who is very nearly as extraordinary as you?

WARNING: The narcissist who makes the "choice" to parent is strongly advised to have *one child and one child only*. Exceeding this limit will impose unmanageable demands on your time, finances, and personal training schedule, while conferring no additional gain.

Challenge 1: Getting Pregnant

The bad news is: the procedures required to achieve a pregnancy are so onerous that they might well be an "undress rehearsal" for the even more oppressive process of raising a child. Just as ontogeny recapitulates phylogeny, the sex-obliterating, time-and-money-devouring, physically revolting process of impregnation recapitulates the equally abhorrent rigors of parenting.

If you're entering parenthood by coercion, not choice, the good news is: "trying to get pregnant" may actually be your way out. Thanks to ever-multiplying environmental toxins, the increasing "maturity" of pregnancy candidates, and (many experts postulate) the escalating ambivalence of career men and women who fear parenthood's deleterious occupational effects, infertility is at an all-time high. And so, therefore, are your opportunities to escape this understandably unwanted fate. (See tips below for "The Determined Parent-Not-to-Be.")

HOW TO MEET THE CHALLENGE

1. Surrender

If your spouse/domestic partner/coparent-to-be insists on sex as a method of procreation, it's best to "surrender" to his/her will. Then:

- Cite studies that "prove" that the chance of conceiving increases in direct proportion to the number and quality of orgasms experienced (by you).

You've tried long and hard to deny the undeniable, but your last performance review hammered home the truth: your career is going nowhere unless you produce a child. You're not "showing well" at company picnics, Christmas/Hanukkah/Kwanza parties, or management meetings, where your competitors flash photo CDs, bronzed report cards, sometimes even brief appearances by their impeccably styled, perfectly behaved offspring.

Choosing between Botox, a facial peel, and laser dermabrasion was tough enough. Deciding on an impregnation approach is more challenging still. The old-fashioned method has its appeal—principally its cost- and time-effectiveness—but the high-tech approach is so much more "this-millennium." Burdened by this decision, you place it in the hands (and other body parts) of your spouse. "If you can't trust me with a child," you explain, "how can you trust me with a choice?"

- Remind him/her of the Seventy-Minute Rule.

- Lie back.

- Enjoy his/her diligent efforts.

Never fear: if current trends hold, your odds of conceiving naturally are about as high as your odds of drawing a glass of pristine water from your kitchen tap. Feign disappointment when this primitive yet enjoyable method proves unproductive. That way, you can have your fake and eat it too.

> **NOTE:** The Narcissist's Sexual Credo, also known as the Seventy-Minute Rule, is spelled out on the *Enough About You*™ Wall Plaque, now available in top-quality waterproof latex for the bargain price of $69.95. Mounted on the bathroom wall, this "necessity, not accessory" will lend inspiration to spontaneous postshower encounters.

"GAYDAR" WARNING TO THE HOMOSEXUAL NARCISSIST:
Here as nowhere else, same-sex couples enjoy a distinct advantage. Unlike your heterosexual counterparts, you need not go through the motions of procreative sex. Unimpeded by social pressures and biological imperative, gay and lesbian couples may simply pass "Go" and advance "straight" to insemination.

2. Let Science Take Its Course
For the narcissist confronted with the prospect of a child, not a choice, the wisdom of proceeding quickly (if not immediately) to high-tech intervention cannot be overstated.

Advantages of the Medical Model of Impregnation

For the Determined Parent-Not-to-Be:

■ Once under the care of a fertility specialist, the narcissist mother-not-to-be will have multiple opportunities to "forget" the dates of doctor's appointments and "mix up" recipes for self-administered hormone injections.

■ If the chosen method is insemination, the father-not-to-be may choose to indulge in two or three "self-love encounters" before surrendering a sample of his (now safely diluted) essence. (See Step Two: Sex, Challenge 1, *Ménage à Un*.)

For the Resigned Parent-to-Be:

■ Medical advances now allow parents to choose their child's gender, IQ, and American Express credit limit even before the sacred moment of conception. To learn how, call the *Enough About You*™ Baby or Not Hotline (details below).

■ The narcissist facing parenthood will need a support system that his/her nanny, cook, and pediatric Rolfer can fall back on during times of exhaustion and isolation. There is simply no better place to build this network than in the waiting room of a prestigious fertility doctor.

■ Casual mention of this doctor's name at your workplace, yoga class, and/or gourmet deli will solidify the high regard in which others hold you, enhancing your ability to support your child in the style to which s/he will quickly become accustomed.

WARNING: While undergoing conception efforts, authentic or otherwise, *don't tell anyone you're "trying."* Narcissists don't try. Narcissists succeed. If your efforts come to fruition, be sure to specify that your pregnancy was planned (narcissists don't have accidents) and how "effortlessly" it happened.

NOTE: For a full discussion of the many methods of conception and conception avoidance suitable for the Superior Self-Lover, call the *Enough About You*™ Baby or Not Hotline at 1–900–BELLY–UP. Calls will be billed to your Visa, MasterCard, or corporate American Express card at a rate of $2.75/minute. Call now; "operators" are standing by.

3. Adopt

The word "adoption" brings a curl to the lip of even the most inexperienced narcissist, and for good reason. Parenting a child not composed of your own DNA eliminates what few excuses there are for raising a child at all. The pitfalls of adoption include, but are not limited to, the following:

- You search the world over for an exceptionally beautiful child, only to be denied credit for his/her impeccable bone structure.

- You risk your hard-earned reputation: others may suddenly see you as a do-gooder who "found a personal solution to the problem of overpopulation" or "rescued babies from unsavory countries and/or neighborhoods."

- You gaze, day after day, into the eyes of a demanding, ungrateful dependent who may act just like you but will never, ever look like you.

Adoption *does* have its advantages, however. It engenders no stretch marks, labor pains, or purchases of hideous maternity clothes. If you've married well, you should be able to afford the purchase of a top-quality child, eliminating chance from the reproductive equation. And if—despite the excellent example you've set, despite everything you've done for him/her—the child should ever misstep, threatening to humiliate you, you need only shrug and blame it on his/her genes.

Challenge 2: Giving Birth

"Thanks" to feminism, there is simply no good way to give birth today. Before the advent of the perversely named "women's health movement," husbands sat peacefully in hospital lobbies reading fishing magazines while doctors mercifully knocked women unconscious at the onset of labor, then woke them the next day with a clean, lovely baby wrapped in gender-appropriate garments. This is no longer possible. If you give birth in today's postfeminist world, you will be made to suffer. And you may take no comfort from childbirth's end: the misery of labor is merely nature's way of preparing you for the lifetime of dirty diapers, sleepless nights, and incessant whining (your child's; yours) you may now anticipate.

HOW TO MEET THE CHALLENGE

1. Leave Nothing to Chance

Childbirth is a momentous event in a woman's life—one from which it may take hours, even days to recover. As difficult as it is for

You're seven months pregnant. Your obstetrician tells you it's time to discuss your "birth options." Sitting in her office, doing a remarkable imitation of a chartreuse VW Beetle, you think, "Now you tell me it's an option?" Your doctor asks if you'd like to be referred to a doula or a midwife, if you'd like to use the birthing center, and what kind of "interventions" will be acceptable to you during the birth.

Should you ask for what you really want: to be knocked out *now* and awakened for your baby's graduation from Yale? No. As usual, your emotions, and you yourself, would be horribly misunderstood. Instead, you go for early accrual of "good mother" points, answering demurely, "I want whatever's best for the baby," knowing that you can—and will—change your tune (to a howling shriek) at the first twinge of labor.

the busy narcissist (and is there any other kind?) to fit childbirth into her life, it becomes virtually impossible when the timing is left to nature. Explain this to your obstetrician; request a scheduled birth. If she proves obstinate, whip out your *Enough About You*™ Personal Data Organizer. Point out your appointments with the colorist, booked two years in advance; the masseuse who comes to your office every Thursday; the weekly trysts with your lover, without which your marriage would simply be intolerable. Remind her that God wouldn't have invented personal data organizers if S/He didn't want women to control their destinies.

NOTE: Once you and your doctor have agreed on the blessed date, enter it in the *Enough About You*™ Personal Data Organizer, the only PDA recognized by MAAMAA (Maternal Afterbirth Activist Matrix of American Assertives). Now available with matching More Than *Enough About You*™ Diaper Bag, $49.95.

2. Just Say Yes

Feminism may have abolished a woman's right to choose the most desirable state in which to experience childbirth—unconsciousness—but fortunately, the far more influential pharmaceutical industry has left a few possibilities open. There are drugs available for women in the throes of childbirth. Good ones. A bit of predelivery coaching will prepare your birthing partner to demand the right drugs at the

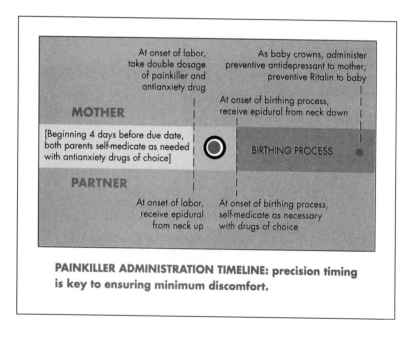

PAINKILLER ADMINISTRATION TIMELINE: precision timing is key to ensuring minimum discomfort.

right time in the right quantities—for both of you. (While the mother of his/her child is writhing in pain, there's no reason for the husband/domestic partner to endure that anguish without a little "better living through chemistry" of his/her own.)

3. Once Is (More Than) Enough

As awful as childbirth is—and despite the banalities that roll like jujubes from the lips of your pathologically cheerful Lamaze instructor, it is *awful*—remember (and remind your spouse, your doctor, your doula, your midwife, your personal birth trainer, your birthing stylist, the nurses, and everyone else within screaming range): no matter how many postpartum sympathy credits you accrue; no matter how many tasteful yet abundant postpartum bouquets are delivered (even by wildly attractive delivery persons); no matter how much fresh admiration your new status earns you from your boss, your Pilates classmates, your mother, or the people who now surrender their seats to you when you're forced to take public transportation—*you will never, ever, do this again.*

Challenge 3: Having a Life

Responsibility. Attachment. Unconditional, heart-swelling adoration. Endless baby talk. All enjoyable experiences to share with yourself, *but now you're expected to have these experiences with another person.* Forever.

It's not just the future that's inconceivable (so to speak). Your daily life, once a sequence of pleasure-seeking activities evocative of *Martha Stewart Living,* now more closely resembles Dante's

Inferno—complete with spontaneous emissions of repulsive substances that you never knew existed, from anatomical regions (yours; your child's) you've always preferred to ignore. You've lost control of your body, your schedule, your career, your white linen down-filled couch. When you try to calm yourself with meditation, the mantra you find yourself chanting is "Flee Here Now."

Follow that instinct. Just as flight attendants advise parents to don oxygen masks before assisting their children, you can provide good care for your child only if you first provide it for yourself. If you can't trust your own instincts, follow the advice of those who know you best. As your spouse, your therapists, your pediatrician, and your pedicurist suggest often, the best thing you can do for your child is to leave him/her in the care of others.

HOW TO MEET THE CHALLENGE

1. Throw Money at the Problem

When you're on your deathbed (or your cryogenicist's), will you regret the paltry sum you spent to make your son or daughter's childhood meaningful, nurturing, and happy (for you)? Or are you more likely to regret skimping on expenditures that could have made his/her life complete (for you)?

Far too many parents today have skewed priorities, and our nation is suffering for their mistakes. Remember, there is no expense that cannot be justified when it comes to your family's well-being. Take out loans if you must. Sign your child up with a modeling agency if you've designed or selected him/her well. Do

You awaken to the muffled sound of a baby's cries. Your bedside Bose Wave™ reads 3:32 A.M. "I just can't do this *again*," you moan silently. But you must. And so you do: endure the ninety seconds or more it takes for the nanny to awaken and tend to your baby's needs.

Several hours later, as you're performing your morning ablutions, you notice something that wasn't there yesterday: the unmistakable beginning of bags beneath your eyes. You're a parent now, a role model for your child. You cannot allow this warning sign to go unheeded. You pull out your *Enough About You*™ Personal Data Organizer and jot down your to-do items for the day: (1) insist that the nanny eliminates that exhausting lag time; (2) make an appointment with your naturopathic dermatologist; and (3) spend the weekend at a nice B&B in the country—*alone*—to catch up on the sleep that is so often denied the new parent.

whatever it takes to provide the psychological, spiritual, and practical necessities that are the birthright of every child's parent.

2. Be a "Good Enough Mother"

Sure, you've got your therapists on speed dial, your career on hold, fifteen extra pounds on your hips, and stains on every piece of clothing and furniture you own. But you've had your child for months, perhaps years, and s/he's still alive—proof positive that you're doing the best you can. You can and should feel good about that.

Parental Bill of Rights

Every child's parent deserves:

- Decent housing, decorated and cleaned weekly by bonded professionals.

- Enough to eat, prepared by talented chefs.

- Access to all support services necessary to make parenthood the rich, satisfying experience it should be, but so rarely is.

Did your parents make mistakes? Of course they did. And look how perfectly you turned out! So later, when your child's therapist "invites" you to daily family sessions (times being what they are, this is as predictable as your Cartier tank keeping time), bring your attorney along to the first session where she will invoke the Good Enough Mother defense.

NOTE: The *Good Enough About You*™ Mother's Defense Kit, $99.95, contains everything your attorney will need to take sworn testimony from your parents, your herbalist, your "friends," your personal shopper, and other experts who can attest that you are indeed "doing the best you can."

3. Teach Your Child(ren) Well

Whatever anyone—including your own child—says about your parenting style, you can rest secure in knowing that time will prove the wisdom of your ways. Someday way too soon, when s/he has narcissist children of his/her own, your son or daughter will thank you for instilling in him/her the superior values, taste, and worldview that has made you/him/her the exceptional human being that you/s/he is. And when your ex-son- or -daughter-in-law suggests otherwise, steel yourself against their unjust accusations: simply download the latest version of the *Good Enough About You*™ Mother's Defense Kit, available online at www.justlikeme.con.

Career

What Size Is Your Parachute?: Only YOU Know the Power of Your Earning Potential

No discussion of narcissists and work can begin without stating the obvious: we shouldn't have to do it.

In more refined societies, contributions like ours are recognized *and subsidized* by governments, educational institutions, and private benefactors. Even in the United States, artists-in-residence are funded to spend weeks, months, years in their studios, creating works of art for the benefit of the greater good.

Narcissists are, in ourselves, such works of art. The labor we expend each day for the greater good—primping in our "studios," readying ourselves to regale the world with our inner and outer beauty—is comparable (speaking modestly now) to the travails of those who repair our streets, teach our children, and liposuct the fat from our thighs. In a more enlightened time and place, the effort we put into maintaining our physical, spiritual, and sartorial splendor—all so that our dazzling light may light the way for others—would be considered work enough. Sadly, in our crass, shortsighted culture, there is no compensation for what we so generously give. Much as our nation needs one, America has no Narcissist Laureate.

And so we are thrust, like common OPs, into the oh-so-aptly-named "workforce." What narcissist would *choose* to enter this dreary, standardized universe, with its inglorious "affirmative" this and "equal" that? Now that CEOs of multinational corporations—the most appropriate job choice for the properly self-assessed narcissist—have come under such undue scrutiny, there is a dearth of jobs that allow for the outward manifestation of our extraordinary inner power. The best jobs, frankly, are taken; even the wiliest narcissist might have a hard time unseating Bill Gates, Madonna, or Michael Jordan.

The fundamental career conflict faced by the narcissist, then, is as simple as it is cruel. We don't want to work. We shouldn't have to work. But bad things happen to the best people. So work we must.

Challenge 1: Working for Someone Else

Unlike the OP, who can say, "I work for the Post Office," and mean it, the true narcissist would never do *anything*—least of all expend our precious labor power—"for" someone else. The narcissist's very purpose on earth, the essential lesson that we were put here to teach, is clearly enunciated in the title of Dr. Phil's best-selling book *Self Matters*. The narcissist would only add the question, "What else does?"

Certainly not a life lived for another—be they deity (see Step One: Spirituality), spouse (see Step Three: Marriage), or employer. The dynamic of dominance and submission inherent in the employer-employee relationship is acceptable to the narcissist in two—and only two—milieus: in the bedroom (with the narcissist in the dominant position), and in the boardroom (with the narcissist in the dominant position). The narcissist's rugged independence and irrepressible self-esteem makes him or her a poor candidate for the role of employee.

Ever since you were thrown off the high school cheerleading team (you were just kicking your highest; you didn't *mean* to give the *unfairly appointed* team captain a concussion), you knew you would always "kick too high" to be a mere "team player." Sure enough, forced by the rising cost of Manolo Blahniks to take a job, you now find yourself indentured to an insensitive, hostile boss. At your performance review, she pointedly crossed the word "performance" off the form; cut your expense account in half (you explained that you needed something to *wear* to those business lunches, but as usual she wouldn't listen); and once again refused your request for a Roche-Bobois–furnished corner office.

Your job reminds you of the food they serve at those "Business as a Team Sport" seminars your boss makes you go to: terrible, and in such small portions. Not only do you hate your job, your boss, and the whole dreary wage slave routine—you can't even count on keeping your job, because you're so unappreciated and misunderstood.

As freedom fighters through the ages have said, "Tis better to die on your feet than to live on your knees." The narcissist would add only this observation: "It's best to stay off your feet entirely, reclining for as much of the day as possible."

HOW TO MEET THE CHALLENGE

Live Beyond Your Means

The most powerful weapon in the narcissist's arsenal is our high self-regard. This is what makes us who we are; this is what distinguishes us from the lowly OP. When forced to labor under inhumane, ego-crushing conditions, the narcissist must maintain his or her morale—and reputation for fine living—at all costs. Think (and talk and spend) like the winner you are, and a winner you will be.

- You've got plastic. Use it. God wouldn't have invented credit cards, mortgages, and car payments if S/He didn't want you to have a little help keeping your spirits—and your reputation—aloft during potentially demoralizing life situations.

- Until your "superiors" come to their senses and promote you to your rightful position, apply a little "lip gloss" when describing the position you're in.

if your title is	say it's
Sales clerk	Commodities trader
if your title is	say it's
Cosmetologist	Cosmologist (you can always say they heard you wrong)
if your title is	say it's
Cocktail waitress	Runway model
if your title is	say it's
FedEx driver	International Communications Facilitator
if your title is	say it's
Rehab patient	Pharmacology Associate
if your title is	say it's
Crossing guard	Transportation Director
if your title is	say it's
Hot dog vendor	Guru (explain that you make your clients "one with everything")

2. Keep Your Eyes on the Prize

The history books are full of stories like yours: great thinkers and doers whose gifts went unrecognized until late in their lives (or even later). When suffering the daily indignities associated with vocational misplacement, it may help the narcissist to keep the historical perspective in mind:

- Van Gogh was ridiculed and scorned.

- Joan of Arc was burned at the stake.

- Michael Jordan was cut from his high school basketball team.

- Steve Jobs was fired from Apple.

Remember: no matter how low on the totem pole you may momentarily seem to be, you're always just one jump shot away from starring in your own Gatorade commercial. And regardless of who signs your paycheck, you report only to a higher power: the one you see in the mirror several hundred times each day.

> **NOTE:** When ambushed by a rare moment of insecurity, the Self-Loving Person (SLP) can regain his or her equilibrium by immersing him/herself in the self-love message, best expressed by the *Enough About You*™ seven-cassette ($49.95) or three-CD ($59.95) set "Free to Be . . . SLP."

3. Sleep with Your Boss

It bears repeating that for the proactive narcissist, working is always the option of last resort—an inconvenient but necessary pit stop on the road to the lifestyle you deserve. While you're traveling that winding highway, a "layover" with your boss at a tasteful yet out-of-the-way hotel might be just the thing to "jump-start" the next phase of your career.

If your boss is otherwise engaged (or better yet, otherwise married), his/her guilt (and/or your understated yet consistent threats) will keep the raises and promotions coming. If your boss is available for an even more lucrative arrangement, go directly to Challenge 3, "Don't Work—Work It." Do not pass "Go"; do not collect $200. Your hand in domestic partnership is worth a lot more than that.

> NOTE: The *Enough About You*™ Guide to Hideaway Hotels describes the mattress quality, in-room erotic movie selection, and confidentiality ratings of hotels, motels, and bed-and-no-breakfasts on the shadowy outskirts of most major metropolitan areas. All accommodations tryst-tested by Mimi E. Gotist herself. "Hard" cover $24.95. "Soft" cover, $15.95, includes one dose of Viagra. Updated information available at www.screwyourboss.organ.

Challenge 2: Working for Yourself

The best thing about self-employment is that you'll never have to worry about being unappreciated again. The worst thing about self-employment is that unless you actually do something, no one will appreciate—or pay—you again.

Narcissists are expert at taking initiative in a crisis. At the first sign of a wrinkle, a mistake in the bank's favor, a going-out-of-business sale, we spring into action, mobilizing all available resources (our own as well as others') to get the job done. Champion sprinters, we are admittedly more challenged by a marathon—for example, the un-remitting effort required to procure, perform, and secure a steady stream of income-producing work. Everything in us cries, "Why?" at the notion of soliciting what we need from others, when others should rightfully be begging to anticipate and meet *our* every need.

Finally, they pushed you too far. Outraged by the mistreatment inflicted on you by your last boss (and the one before that, and the one before that), you've "moved on to pursue other opportunities" more suited to your self-sufficient nature.

You've started your own business, and you're doing everything right. You've rented and renovated a spacious office in the hottest neighborhood in town, hired an attractive yet competent staff, and retained the artist who created the Nike swoosh to design your logo. To build employee motivation and retention, you offer unparalleled salary and benefits (to yourself, that is; your staff is so much better at making do than you are).

But those "other opportunities" have yet to materialize. The bills are stacking up like dim sum plates at Sunday brunch. And you're fairly certain that it isn't your decorator who removed all the designer furniture from the lobby.

HOW TO MEET THE CHALLENGE

1. Be the Boss You Never Had

Don't blame yourself for your predicament. You wouldn't be in it if you'd had the kind of employer you deserve: one with the warmth, compassion, and patience it takes to bring out the best in a person like you. So what if your period of adjustment lasted one year, or five? Who's to say you wouldn't have turned the corner the day after you were summarily asked to "resign"?

Never having been well bossed yourself, it may be difficult to give yourself the bossing you need.

- Start by listing the things your ideal Good Boss would have done for you.

- Amass the resources (your own and others') needed to give yourself what should rightly have been given to you long, long ago.

ADVANCED EXERCISE: Once you feel confident that you've overcome past hurts and become a Good Boss to yourself, you may then attempt to offer this gift to others. Begin with your second-most-valued employee. Closely monitor impact. Don't hesitate to retreat to bossing only yourself if desired results are not immediately achieved.

WARNING: The deprivation you've suffered may have driven your longings deep underground. Summon them slowly, beginning with basics like "effusive praise" before attempting the more challenging "two months of paid vacation."

2. Charge More, Work Less

Ordinary Persons call it "freelancing"; narcissists know that self-employment is anything but "free." Rather, it offers the unique opportunity to charge, finally, what we're worth—and to exercise our innate creativity in the billing process as well.

The burden of self-employment must be borne by one of two parties: the employer or the employed. Given the value that we add to our clients' ventures, we richly deserve to be compensated for keeping ourselves warm in winter, cool in summer, current with

MIMI E. GOTIST • DILETTANT AT LARGE 1 My Way, Or-the-highway, CA 94111	**MIMI E. GOTIST • DILETTANT AT LARGE** 1 My Way, Or-the-highway, CA 94111

INVOICE

Expense Item	Amount
Pedicure ....$	75.
Napping (creative downtime) ....200.	
Lunch (food for thought) ....48.	
Air conditioning ....180.	
One hour actual work ....90.	
Bottle of wine for creative flow ......390.	
Full-body massage.......................115.	

TOTAL	**$1,098.**

payable upon receipt

INVOICE

_____

TOTAL = $1,500.
payable yesterday

the IRS, and well groomed at all times. Rather than sullying client relationships negotiating "air conditioning fees" and "pedicure costs," we can make our "expensive-lancing" fruitful for all concerned by building those costs into our pricing structure—giving our clients an effortless way to demonstrate the appreciation they may otherwise have difficulty expressing.

3. Sleep with Your Client(s)

See Challenge 1, Solution 3, "Sleep with Your Boss."

Challenge 3: Don't Work—Work It

As the timelessly trendy philosopher Kahlil Gibran wrote so pre-sciently, years before laser eye surgery was even a possibility, "Work is love made visible." In order for the narcissist to love his/her work, it must be deeply meaningful; it must advance a cause in which the worker deeply believes. For narcissists, there can be no cause more meaningful than that of our own advancement—straight to the vocational mountaintop, where meaningful work is done only by others.

Where else, indeed, would the narcissist aspire to be? The most accomplished among us have transcended the very paradigm of "career." We have staff. We have "interests." We engage only in full-time self-care that is arranged, implemented, and funded by the efforts of others.

There are but three paths to this hallowed ground: successful entrepreneurship, inheritance, and marriage/divorce.

HOW TO MEET THE CHALLENGE

1. Succeed in Business Without Really Trying

Starting a business involves many tasks that the narcissist will find onerous: writing a business plan, raising capital, paying for lunch, and most stressful of all, coming up with an original idea.

But why go to the trouble of conceiving something new, when so many perfectly fine ideas already exist? In the noble tradition of those who adopt children as a remedy for overpopulation and those who buy recycled materials and then recycle them again, the

You have moved your cheese, and everyone else's. You have sweated the small stuff, the big stuff, and all the stuff in between. You have memorized the ten secrets of success. You can recite the seven habits of highly effective people in five languages, including Pig Latin. You have managed others in one- and three-minute increments. You have unfurled the parachute of your dreams over endless fields of dreams. Now you ask yourself the same question the barista poses each morning when you order your lowfat decaf triple-shot latte: "Why bother?" All that effort, and you still have not one measly million to your name.

So you take the next step: you write—and live—a career/marriage guidebook of your own: *Do Who Makes Money, and If the Love Follows, Better Yet.*

narcissist in search of a Boom of One's Own can "adopt" and "recycle" the unused business concepts of others.

- In any city worthy of a narcissist's taxes, there are "business incubators" where entrepreneurs meet, network, and share their new business ideas. Join one.

- Meet. Network. Take notes.

- Retain the services of an excellent attorney.

- "Adopt" and "recycle" the best idea(s) you hear.

- If necessary, move to the next city worthy of a narcissist's taxes.

2. Inherit Well

This time-honored method of avoiding work entirely is the most desirable—and sadly, the most inaccessible. Narcissists of "a certain age" are likely to be rebuffed in their attempts to be adopted by billionaires. Even the young among us will find it challenging to identify, and make themselves attractive to, families listed in the Social Register who are in the market for heirs. If you haven't come by an inheritance in the traditional manner, you may want to access it instead via marriage/divorce (see below).

3. Marry/Divorce Well

As Kahlil Gibran would say, were he alive and writing self-help bestsellers today, "Love is work made unnecessary." If fate has been unkind to you, forcing you to eke out a living without benefit of benefactor or trust fund, marriage/divorce may be your most desirable Plan B.

- Marry well.

- Divorce better.

- Write and sell a memoir and movie rights to your successful experience. Call it *The One-Minute Marryer.*

Health and Fitness

My Body, My Self: The Narcissistic Wound Doesn't Have to Hurt (You)

Although narcissists appear to be paragons of physical perfection, it's what doesn't show that hurts (us, and those we've chosen to minister to us). Plagued with ailments that those who claim to care for us coldly write off as "psychosomatic" or "pitiful attempts at attention-getting," we are in fact excruciatingly sensitive (some would say "high-strung") instruments. Much as the Stradivarius resonates to the maestro's gentlest touch, our bodies register the subtlest sensation. The aches, pains, and seemingly insignificant symptoms that elude the Ordinary Person are felt all too profoundly by such finely tuned individuals as we.

If the OP's body is his temple, the narcissist's is the Taj Mahal—a wonder of the world, delighting all who behold its ageless splendor. Although the narcissist alone bears the burden of maintaining, decorating, and refurbishing this font of public pleasure, others hypocritically accuse us of spending inordinate amounts of time, effort, and money on what they refer to as "frivolous luxuries"—necessities, actually, for this altruistic project of continual beautification.

Just as pregnant women are said to be "eating for two," narcissists who spend their hard-earned (or hard-inherited, or hard-married/divorced) money on these "luxuries" are actually liposuctioning, dieting, and StairMastering for us all. Yet narcissists receive little if any financial, practical, spiritual, or moral support for this generous undertaking—an injustice that is doubly ironic, since in this case beauty is truly in the "I" of the beholder.

Challenge 1: Inept Health "Professionals"

The fundamental anguish of the narcissist, simply put, is that we are so utterly misunderstood. (Our detractors refer to this as the "narcissist wound," as if to imply that the flaw resides in *us.*) Our self-love is misinterpreted as conceit, our self-respect as arrogance, our righteous needs as pathological. Day after day we endure this injury stoically, concealing our disappointment with remarkable self-restraint. But when it comes to the care of our bodies, this problem may be life-threatening, and therefore must be addressed head (and mouth) on.

Unwilling, unable, and/or uninsured to deal with the narcissist's exceptional self-awareness, many health practitioners (and they *do* seem to be practicing on us, don't they?) reject our efforts to partner in what should be the joint venture of maintaining an exemplary body. Putting their own egos before ours (as if they, or anyone,

You've gained two pounds for absolutely no reason. As if that weren't terrifying enough, you've been having bad hair days all week. Your doctor has become so unresponsive (at your last appointment she "suggested" you wait until you've been symptomatic for a year or more before calling her again) that you decide to take responsibility for your own healing. You call in sick; use your time in seclusion to do some online research. (You wouldn't *dare* go out in your condition.)

Masterfully navigating your *Enough A-Byte You*™ Titanium PowerBroker, you cruise the medical self-care sites. Weight gain—check. Limp hair—check. Fatigue—yes! This explains why you've fallen asleep before the "Order" segment of *Law and Order* for the last three nights in a row.

Panicked now, you call your doctor. She reminds you that she tested you thoroughly the *last* time you gained a pound, and refuses to authorize a workup. You remind *her* that this isn't the first time you've suffered from her neglect. Last week, when you noticed that still-undiagnosed growth on your face, she insisted it was a *pimple*.

could get away with *that!*), they resent our gift for self-vigilance, the consistency of our self-reporting. In fact, they should be grateful that we do so much of their work for them, often diagnosing our own ailments before they are visible to the naked (or tastefully gown-draped) eye.

NOTE: The *Enough A-Byte You*™ Titanium PowerBroker computer, $2,695.00, comes preset with the only screen-saver you'll need: a self-cleaning mirror. Double rows of flattering, low-watt vanity lights frame the monitor's edge, suffusing you in a gentle ambient glow, so you'll look your best for Internet "cruising" and killer makeup apps.

HOW TO MEET THE CHALLENGE

1. Take Stock

With today's health "care" what it is, your best hedge against dying early and alone is to take ownership of your life, and invest in your well-being, by taking ownership of a few well-chosen stocks. The

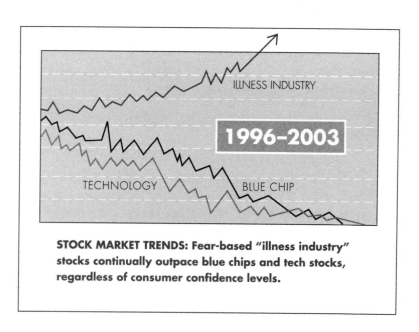

STOCK MARKET TRENDS: Fear-based "illness industry" stocks continually outpace blue chips and tech stocks, regardless of consumer confidence levels.

economy may rise and fall, but pharmaceuticals, medical "insurance," and monthly full-body diagnostic MRIs are here to stay. Owning a piece of the booming illness industry might not save your life, but it'll help you achieve the kind of "personal growth" that makes life, death, and everything in between a lot more pleasant to endure.

2. Change Doctors Early and Often

Far too innovative to accept conventional wisdom, narcissists sneer at such worn-out, New Age platitudes as "You can't change anyone else; you can only change yourself." We can, and should, change our doctors—about as often as we change our sheets. (Be sure to bring your own gown each time you visit a new medical office; most provide gowns so tacky they'll make you even sicker than you already are.)

You'll know you've waited too long to switch if your doctor demonstrates even one of these warning signs of callous disregard:

- S/he refuses to refer you to a specialist.

- S/he refers you to a psychiatrist.

- S/he refers you to the local theater group.

- S/he gives you a thick sheaf of handouts on hypochondria, Munchausen syndrome, and psychosomatic illness.

CALENDAR | IT'S A GOOD-FOR-ME THING™

SUN	MON	TUE	WED	THURS	FRI	SAT
call ex—alimony now past due 1	change doctors 2	craft new mailbox out of old soup cans 3	find Third World goods manufacturer 4	find low-rent retailer to peddle goods 5	fire a random staff member 6	tape TV special: "Cooking the Books" 7
have sex with José 8	change doctors 9	have José re-paint garden shed 10	craft center-piece with old printer cartridges 11	review shed paint job; show José errors 12	fire José 13	plant spring bulbs 14
start magazine; name after self 15	change doctors 16	interview/sleep with potential assistants 17	rotate dishes 18	fire a random staff member 19	build higher fence around property 20	FedEx gift-wrapped dog poo to ex 21
get full-body "massage" from José 22/29	change doctors 23/30	burn all CDs and clothes left behind by ex 24	scour home for new do-it-someone-else project 25	refill Rxs; store in meds cellar 26	host dinner party; revel in guests' envy 27	craft "No Trespassing" sign with hot-glue gun 28

3. Sue

Even for the narcissist, suing for malpractice is the remedy of last resort. Use it only if:

- You've exhausted all other options.

- Your attorney is on retainer and you'd like to get your money's worth, for once.

When you must sue, know that you do so not just for yourself, but in the name of the teeming masses: OPs lacking the wherewithal to defend themselves against overscheduled, overpaid doctors who don't bother to learn their patients' names, let alone their favorite magazines. (What worse example of "malpractice" could there be than leaving you in a polyester-upholstered waiting room full of cheaply framed mall art and two-year-old issues of *Golf Digest?*)

Challenge 2:
Inept Fitness "Professionals"

Where is the rocket science in the mission of the fitness professional: to fine-tune the precision tool that is the narcissist's body? But incompetence runs rampant throughout the industry, and so you are driven from health club to yoga studio, from kickboxing master to personal Spinning trainer—all to no avail. Despite the earnestness of your quest, the sinews of supple muscle that should swell beneath the silken surface of your skin remain hidden beneath the very flesh that you pay these "experts" to eliminate. They try to distract you, driveling on and on about inner beauty. What you're looking for, you retort, is *thinner beauty*.

Adding insult to injury, these minions offer heart-rate charts, "inspirational" quotes from Jane Fonda and Richard Simmons, and admonitions against the one thing that gives you reason to live (dessert). If you wanted to study physiology, you'd be dating a doctor. If you wanted to "work it," you'd be flirting, not exercising. If

You're meeting with your fourth personal trainer in as many weeks, and already she's making the same faux pas as her predecessors: interrogating you about your diet, your daily routines, your *weight*—as if you'd discuss that with *anyone*. Doesn't she understand the motivational value of the well-phrased compliment? Couldn't she comment on your determination, your courage, your brand-new Donna Karan workout togs—or offer a bit of historical perspective? In a more civilized era, you'd be posing for Rubens instead of being scrutinized in the glare of floor-to-ceiling mirrors by a hyperactive twig wearing *Nike*.

You're still trying to make this relationship work—fishing for compliments, having her remove the price tag you "forgot" to cut off your new Prada sweatshirt—when she pulls out a bottle of water. *Domestic, supermarket-brand water.* Your worst suspicions about her confirmed, you pack up your Kate Spade gym bag and go home.

you wanted to *sweat* . . . well, you can't even *imagine* the circumstances that would make you want to do something as unattractive and unpleasant as that.

HOW TO MEET THE CHALLENGE

1. Hire a Role Model, Not a Runway Model

In order to grow up with hopes and dreams, children need to see successful people who look like them in their classrooms and communities. Similarly, the narcissist undertaking a fitness regime needs a personal trainer who looks like him/her—only much, much worse. Working out beside a sculpted jock born to genetic mutants with zero body fat and ideal height-to-weight ratio will only discourage you from following your fitness path. To ensure success, hire a trainer who weighs at least twice as much, and looks no more than half as good, as you do.

2. Set Realistic Goals

Ordinary Persons have no life. Therefore, they have nothing better to do with their time and money than to fritter it away in a gym. They have no aesthetic bar to lower by perspiring or flushing in public, no reputation to risk by being seen at the wrong yoga class or gym. A "fitting" fitness plan for the narcissist must encompass all of these factors, while adhering to the Narcissist Imperative: put out half the effort, achieve double the results.

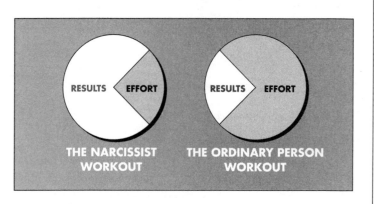

RESULTS ⟨ EFFORT   RESULTS ⟩ EFFORT

**THE NARCISSIST
WORKOUT**   **THE ORDINARY PERSON
WORKOUT**

**THE NARCISSIST IMPERATIVE: put out half the effort,
achieve double the results. Result is exact inverse of
the OP ratio.**

3. Sue

An implicit expectation of trust exists between the narcissist and
the person(s) to whom she acknowledges her imperfections, however minor. Allowing that trust to be violated is a psychological
as well as physical risk that no self-loving person can afford to
take.

If you've tried everything else with the offending member of
your fitness staff—listened patiently to his unreasonable demands
(for example, that you eat less and exercise more), accommodated
her refusal to empty the gym so you can work out in privacy (until
you start to achieve the desired results, at which point you'll demand

the presence of an admiring crowd), allowed him not one, not two, but *three days* to deliver the promised results—you have no recourse but legal action. If s/he protests, just assure him/her firmly that you're doing exactly what s/he's been telling you to do: going for "the burn."

Challenge 3: Inept Beauty "Professionals"

Few professionals (or amateurs, for that matter) can have as devastating an impact on your life as those to whom you entrust the portico of your soul, the tongue-and-groove of your temple: your physical appearance. Even the most rigorous screening procedures will not suffice when it comes to selecting the artists who style and color your hair; shape and polish your nails; slash, burn, and exfoliate your skin.

Soliciting referrals from fellow narcissists—the method of choice for making such lesser selections as those of spouse (see Step Three: Marriage), child (Step Four: Parenting), or cellphone plan—is simply too dangerous in this case. Consider the consequences. If the reference is a good one, the Referring Narcissist can and will take partial credit for your enhanced beauty. If the referral is a bad one, the ramifications can be graver still.

> **WARNING:** The Revenge Referral is a cruel yet common way for vindictive "friends" to win a round of the Get-Back Game. *Avoid at all costs.*

> **FBI WARNING:** If you are offered an unsolicited beauty referral via phone, e-mail, or any other long-distance

transmission, *you may be the victim of an interstate fashion crime.* Report immediately to the FBI as well as the NBBB (Narcissists' Best Business Bureau).

There is only one safe criterion to use when selecting your staff of beauty professionals: hire the ones who charge the most. Even if their work is disappointing (and whose, besides yours, isn't?), you'll benefit from dropping their names later, when you mention the legal action you're taking against them (see Challenge 3 below).

You wake up hung over. There's a sinking feeling in your stomach, and something tells you it's not just the margaritas. You reach up to brush the hair out of your eyes. And find that there is none there.

Now you remember what you were drinking to forget: that horrific haircut you got yesterday. You check the clock, wonder if you should bother calling in "hideous." You're tempted to stay in bed with the covers over your head—concealing, if not destroying, the evidence. But then your inner adult tells you, "You're good enough, you're smart enough, and doggone it, people like you don't deserve haircuts like this." So you gather your courage, tuck what's left of your locks under an oversized yet chic *chapeau,* and return to the scene of the crime. You demand your money back, insist on a "repair cut," and get it—a well-executed case of rage before beauty.

HOW TO MEET THE CHALLENGE

1. Prepare for the Worst-Case Scenario

No matter how carefully you select your facialist, laserist, or Botoxist, these treatments may still render you unpresentable for days, weeks, or months. (Whoever coined the phrase "Beauty is only skin deep" never had a truly awful facial.) Despite our good-faith efforts to avoid cosmetic injury, the sad fact is, even narcissists get the bruise. Before undertaking cosmetic enhancement, prepare for this unavoidable scenario by taking the following precautions:

- Insist on a "cosmetic injury" clause in your employment contract, allowing for paid medical leave covering a minimum of ten incidents per calendar year. (Any employer worth working "for" will understand that you can't do business with your bangs too short or your pores hanging open.)

- Stock up on props to smooth the transition: veiled hats to disguise a botched facial; wigs to wear while a bad haircut grows out; closed-toe shoes to conceal a substandard polish choice. (If employed, these items should be covered under your cosmetic injury clause; if self-employed, they qualify as tax-deductible medical expenses.)

- Your professional, psychological, and spiritual well-being depend on your aura of success. Keep an aura therapist on call for emergency adjustments (see cosmetic injury coverage, above).

2. Lie Down for Your Rights

When you retain the services of a new member of your beauty staff, s/he may not realize who you are, or how high the stakes of his/her performance are—for you, and therefore for him/her. Don't wait until you're prone on the waxing table or gritting your teeth in pain under your electrologist's lamp to mention the caliber of the people who will witness and admire your Brazilian bikini line, the prestige boost that his/her practice might enjoy as a result, and the depth of the discount to which all of this surely entitles you.

3. Sue

Bad haircuts do happen to good people, but that's no reason for you to bear the brunt of a beauty professional's carelessness and/or incompetence. God wouldn't have put attorneys on this earth if S/He didn't have a plan for them, and there could hardly be a better use of their time than to win compensation for the bodily injuries you suffer at the hands of those to whom you entrust your greatest asset. Use the formula on the next page to figure the damages.

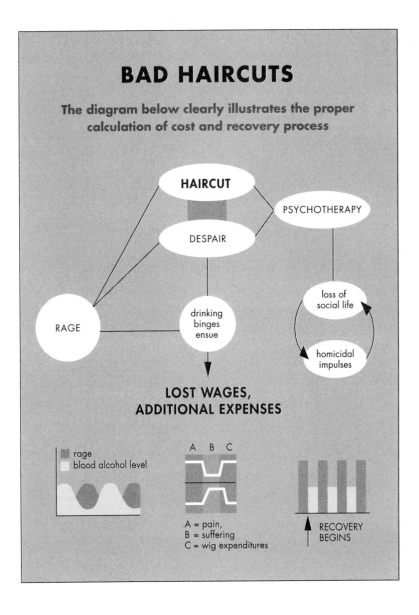

BAD HAIRCUTS

The diagram below clearly illustrates the proper calculation of cost and recovery process

HAIRCUT

PSYCHOTHERAPY

DESPAIR

loss of social life

RAGE

drinking binges ensue

homicidal impulses

LOST WAGES, ADDITIONAL EXPENSES

rage
blood alcohol level

A B C

A = pain,
B = suffering
C = wig expenditures

RECOVERY BEGINS

Personal Growth

I'm Okay, I'm Okay: Getting the Mirroring You Deserve

For the narcissist, self-improvement is a paradoxical proposition. What *about* our selves could we possibly hope to improve? Similarly, the goal of personal growth—self-awareness—is not one to which we have reason to aspire. Who could be more self-aware than the eternally introspective narcissist?

Ordinary Persons look to others for affirmation. Narcissists are all too accustomed to giving it to ourselves. OPs spend a fortune on "confidence-building" and "goal-setting" tapes, books, workshops, and other nothing-to-show-for-it self-help "tools." Narcissists' money is better spent on things (*nice* things, durable things, designer things) that manifest our justifiable self-confidence—while enhancing it. Narcissists know that it is not *our* "issues" standing between us and our admittedly lofty goals, but those of others: those human speed bumps—small people with their petty jealousies and limited imaginations—who try (fruitlessly, but annoyingly) to slow our path to self-fulfillment.

Desperate for help, OPs rely on arcane, unproven methodologies—astrology, numerology, psychotherapy—for advice about their futures and their fates. They think so poorly of themselves that nearly anyone or anything—a workshop on "The Gestalt of Authentic Tantra," for example, or "The Psychosemiotics of Golf"—can actually give their egos a much-needed boost. Narcissists face precisely the opposite challenge. When we hire personal growth "mentors"— therapists, life coaches, stockbrokers—we do so begrudgingly, knowing that they cannot possibly be as intelligent, perceptive, or assertive as we ourselves are.

Why, then, do narcissists participate in the personal growth industry at all? It is perhaps the ultimate proof of the narcissist's humility that despite the apex of human potential that we embody, we strive endlessly to become more perfect still. As Michelangelo is rumored to have said, "There's always room for one more angel on the Sistine Chapel." Always open to adding another "angel," we see ourselves as the never-finished masterpieces that we are.

Challenge 1: Therapy

Therapy offers one thing that narcissists need: uninterrupted, one-way, nonreciprocal attention (albeit at day-spa prices)—and many things that we would much prefer to do without. Therapists promise to "mirror" us, but they spend less time looking at us in a year than we spend looking at ourselves in a day. They "validate" how special we are, then hold us to the very same rules that they impose upon their OPxs (Ordinary Patients). They claim to admire our boundless creativity, then insist on enforcing "boundaries" that constrain our ability to express it: expecting us to make and cancel appointments *hours* in advance, as if we were fortune-tellers, not fortune-seekers; accusing us of having "intimacy issues," then refusing to meet with us in more intimate, true-to-life settings— for a latte, say, or a moonlit walk on the beach. Most hypocritically of all, week after week, at precisely the fifty-minute mark, they say they're "sorry we have to stop now," then expel us from their offices, denying us even the rollover minutes that the better cell-phone plans offer.

Why do narcissists leap these hurdles, write those checks, sit in those waiting rooms reading back issues of *The New Yorker?* Because, despite the risk that we will outdistance others at an even greater pace, *we are that committed to becoming the very best people we can be.* (Or because a judge, a jittery but well-endowed fiancé/fiancée, or an employer under the influence of an organizational dynamics consultant says we have to.)

WARNING: In most major American cities, there are unskilled, unlicensed paraprofessionals who pass themselves off as "personal coaches," "life coaches," or "investment advisers." These psycho-ciphers are best left to corporate executives with bloated "professional development" budgets to spend. Therapy of any sort is unpleasant enough; if you're going to subject yourself to it, go for the real thing.

After six years of twice-weekly psychotherapy sessions, Dr. X knows more about you than your own mother does. (That isn't saying much, as Dr. X has helped you to see.) Dr. X tells you often how well you've turned out, given all that you've had to overcome, and how resilient and optimistic you are, considering. Most tellingly, he laughs heartily at your jokes—even when you don't know you've made one.

Why, then, hasn't Dr. X taken the next step? Why hasn't he asked you out on a date?

As you're pondering this mystery, your years of therapeutic work finally pay off. Empathetically, you realize that Dr. X is intimidated by you, afraid to be rejected by someone as dynamic and evolved as you, his star patient. He's waiting for you to make the first move!

Graciously, you invite Dr. X to have you over for dinner tonight. His reaction isn't what you'd expected. He doesn't fall out of his leather swivel chair, swooning with gratitude, or ask if you'd prefer lobster or a simple tuna tartare. Looking at you impassively, as if you're no more than an Ordinary Patient, he simply murmurs his usual, "Could you say more about that?"

HOW TO MEET THE CHALLENGE

1. Turn Back Time

Cher sang about it; many OPs waste years of their lives looking for ways to do it. By following the steps below, narcissists in therapy can actualize it.

- During your first session, take careful note of your therapist's clock.

- Before your second session, buy an exact replica of that clock. Set it to run fifteen minutes slow.

- During your second session, cry, sneeze, or "nervously" shred all the tissues in the box. When your therapist goes to get you a fresh supply, substitute your clock for hers.

- When your session ends (fifteen satisfying minutes late), tell your therapist that you need to "change your regular time." (You're nothing if not honest.) When she gets up to look through her appointment book, replace your clock with hers.

- Repeat at subsequent sessions.

if your therapist	you should
Catches you in the act of clock replacement	Tell her you were just regressing to your childhood, fifteen minutes at a time

if your therapist	you should
Catches on within the first two sessions	Burst into tears when she confronts you; remind her of how your mother distrusted you too

if your therapist	you should
Takes longer than two sessions to catch on	Find a brighter therapist

ADVANCED EXERCISE: Try the direct approach instead. When your therapist says, "We have to stop now," correct her gently. Say, "Actually, I'm good for another half-hour," and go on talking.

2. Flip the Script

Narcissists make impressive therapy clients. Before long, even the moderately alert therapist will start commenting on this—mentioning how much s/he's learning from working with you, and how "interesting" and even "extraordinary" you are.

Why should you pay for what you're learning from your therapist, when s/he's not paying for what s/he's learning from you? You shouldn't, and you don't have to. Just take these Three Simple Steps™ to balance the scales—or better yet, tip them in your favor.

Step One™: Begin by "sharing your innermost doubts" and suggesting a discounted rate. Example:

Narcissist to Therapist: "It's been six years now, and I don't feel like I've made much progress."

Therapist to Narcissist: "You're not making as much progress as you'd like."

Narcissist to Therapist: "Since you agree that I'm not getting what I'm paying for, can I get 20 percent off?"

Step Two™: Move quickly to suggesting an even exchange that "mirrors" your therapist's experience. Example:

Narcissist to Therapist: "I think I'm finally starting to get better."

Therapist to Narcissist: "You're feeling better. I'm so glad to hear that."

Narcissist to Therapist: "Since I'm making you feel better too, shouldn't we split the fee fifty-fifty?"

Step Three™: Once you've established reciprocity, suggest a financial arrangement that "mirrors" the gestalt of your dynamic.

Narcissist to Therapist: "I'm doing so much better, thanks to you."

Therapist to Narcissist: "You're the one who's done all the work."

Narcissist to Therapist: "I hear what you're saying. So from now on, you'll pay *me*, right?"

3. Date Your Therapist

There are many therapeutic "boundaries" that may be appropriate for OPxs, but are insulting and irrelevant when applied to narcissists—chief among them, the notion that therapists should not be friends (or more) with their clients. Defending this prohibition, therapists cite such false threats as "transference" (in fact, the only thing that gets transferred is $75 to $125 per session from the narcissist's checking account to the therapist's); "countertransference" (difficult, but not impossible, to accomplish; see Step Three™ above); and "trust issues" (the "issue" is simple: if you're lucky enough to start out with a trust fund, it'll be gone by the time you're cured).

For the narcissist client who hasn't yet negotiated a suitable payment arrangement (see Three Simple Steps™ above), dating the therapist can accomplish the same purpose. Once your social relationship has replaced the far more expensive and limiting professional dynamic, you'll be able to benefit from even more frequent contact with your therapist—without the annoying hiss of the white noise machine or that awkward check-writing moment at session's end.

> **WARNING:** If you marry your therapist, jealous "friends" are likely to gossip. Don't let comments like, "No wonder! He *needs* a full-time therapist," or, "You'd *have* to be a shrink to put up with her," get you down. Just ignore them—or hum a few bars of Melissa Etheridge's anthem to unconventional relationships: "I don't care what they say / What do they know about this love anyway?"

Challenge 2: Workshops

Compared to the maximum-level-of-difficulty method of personal growth (see Challenge 1, "Therapy"), self-improvement workshops and seminars are relatively pleasant—and far less draining to the purse *and* the psyche. Many workshops satisfy the requirements of the prescribing physician, judge, lover, or employer as well.

For the most positive experience, avoid public or court-ordered workshops, which are often conducted in strip mall conference rooms, featuring folding metal chairs and weak coffee. Instead, seek

---

Against all odds, your dream has come true: the wedding date is set, the gift list composed, the crash diet under way. There's just one hitch: your intended announces that s/he won't go through with it unless you "work on your issues."

The bad news is, even though s/he demanded it, your fiancé/fiancée won't underwrite the cost of your self-improvement. The good news? Since "for you, therapy could take a lifetime," your beloved decrees that a weekend worship will suffice. Your conjugal clock ticking, you start your search for the workshop that will net the most bang (so to speak) for your prenuptial buck.

"An Inner Journey to Sacred Waikiki"? No—Waikiki is *so* fifties sitcom.

"Longing and Belonging—Attachment Issues and Romantic Love"? The title alone contains even more terrifying words than the wedding vows themselves.

Finally you find the perfect workshop, a two-week "intensive" on "Maintaining the Perennial Border," held on a vineyard in Provence. If your betrothed questions the relevance of the topic, you'll just tell him/her that you're going to work on your "recurring boundary issues."

out high-end, New Age workshops held at four-star hotels and nicely landscaped retreat centers. The food is often excellent (call ahead to make sure you're not stumbling into a hotbed of vegetarianism, or worse), the accommodations top-notch (be sure to book a private room; the last thing you need after a hard day of "breaking into small groups" is to break into another one), and the humiliation mild to moderate (or, if you play your cards right, nonexistent; see "Subvert the Dominant Paradigm" below).

HOW TO MEET THE CHALLENGE

1. Do Unto Others

In today's therapeutically correct world, trying to help others is considered a psychological *faux pas.* This presents a dilemma for narcissists, whose only problems are the problems of those around us. Workshops offer a way out of this seemingly dead-end dynamic. It's *not okay* to suggest therapy for someone else, but it *is* okay to "invite" a friend, spouse, or employee to accompany you to a workshop or seminar. Once there, you can claim the need for some "alone time" to "process the experience," then slip off to the nearest outlet mall. While you're enjoying the only self-improvement you need—some truly therapeutic "retail therapy"—your guest will be undertaking the self-improvements that you want him/her to make.

2. Subvert the Dominant Paradigm

Why should the ever-pioneering narcissist accept conventional parameters of self-help? Instead of trying to fit a round peg (the narcissist) into a square hole (the rigid box of traditional self-improvement), the narcissist can and should design, implement, and/or adapt his/her own personal growth "workshops." Instead of paying hundreds per day to New Age charlatans posing as gurus, you can be your own guru—at the vacation destination of your choice. Even if you must stay close to home, be sure to attend only those workshops certified as narcissist-friendly by WAAWAA (Workshop Attendees' Activist Web of American Assertives).

ordinary person workshop	narcissist workshop
Driving under the influence (DUI)	Striving under the influence (SUI)
Stress management	Dress management ("wardrobe consultation")
Assertiveness training	Assertiveness claiming
Home improvement	Staff improvement
Wellness enhancement	Greatness enhancement
Workplace ergonomics	Workplace egonomics
Psychic healing	Psychic stealing ("intellectual property theft for fun and profit")

3. Those Who Won't, Teach

For the narcissist who must attend a workshop, but rightly rebels at the notion of paying to do so, attending as a teacher instead of a student is a viable, and lucrative, option. True, it's more work—but not much. Just follow the lead of the legions of successful workshop leaders before you:

- Pack as many participants as possible onto convergent cushions crammed onto the floor of a "cozy" room (thereby providing a "provocatively intimate environment" in the cheapest room in the place, while raking in maximum enrollment fees. See "Workshop Fee Guidelines" below).

- Encourage participants to "sit with their feelings and see what comes up" (besides the body heat in the room, and your tax bracket).

- Give the group a one-hour "free-writing exercise." While they're "free-writing," "retreat" to your room for a profoundly self-improving (and well-paid) nap.

ADVANCED EXERCISE: The exceptionally ambitious narcissist may choose to "teach" two workshops concurrently, skillfully synchronizing the "sitting with feelings" and "free-writing exercise" segments of workshops held in adjoining rooms, effectively managing to be in two places (and two profit centers) at one time.

WARNING: Do not attempt this advanced exercise in facilities not properly equipped to handle it. Each "cozy" room must be soundproofed to prevent audible "spillover"; each must have its own bathroom to ensure that students from one group don't inadvertently interact with (i.e., learn of the existence of) the other group.

Workshop Fee Guidelines

Use this formula to establish workshop fees:

$$SR \div \#P + RRF - \$FM = WFPP$$

SR = Site Rating of the space in which the workshop is held (see chart below)

#P = number of Participants

RRF = Room Rental Fee

$FM = value of Free Massage provided by facility

WFPP = Workshop Fee Per Participant

Site Rating Guidelines

(Each martini represents $100 per participant per day)

Unobstructed ocean view ....ΥΥΥΥΥ

Ocean view—whitewater only...ΥΥΥΥΥ

Nature view—including wildlife mammals............................ΥΥΥΥΥ

Nature view—birds and flowers only...................................ΥΥΥΥ

On the grounds of an authentic Buddhist monastery ....ΥΥΥ

On the grounds of a New Age Buddhist monastery...............ΥΥΥΥΥ

Unobstructed parking lot view ....ΥΥ

Parking lot view—Dumpster only...Υ

Challenge 3: Into the Mystic

The metaphysical approach is the self–improvement genre *sans pareil* for the narcissist interested in (or compelled by others to undergo) personal growth. Unlike the far more rigorous disciplines already described, such timeless tools as numerology, astrology, tarot, crystal healing, and sacred geometry entail few, if any, of the dread rules and boundaries that dot the psychotherapeutic minefield. Where rules do exist, those who made them are long dead, and therefore unlikely to enforce them.

These practices offer other advantages as well. Practitioners market themselves honestly, without resorting to the obfuscating

You've paid your personal growth dues so many times over, you've got the local retreat center on payroll deduction. You've been psychoanalyzed and psychotherapized so thoroughly, you couldn't utter a "you message" if your afterlife depended on it. You've been Reiki'd and Rolfed till you were nearly Rune'd. If you were any more in touch with yourself, you'd be collecting disability benefits for repetitive stress injury to your right hand (see Step Two: *Ménage à Un*).

Still, your boss, your spouse, and your therapist insist that you "deal with your issues" if you want to keep your job, your marriage, and your primetime 7 P.M. therapy appointment. So once again—their threats ringing in your ears, their referrals Post-It-ed to your *Enough About You*™ Personal Data Organizer, you set out resentfully in search of yet more self-help.

alphabet soup of initials so prevalent in the self-promotion of therapists and workshop leaders. And metaphysical practitioners promise specific results (compare "inner-child healing" to "astrological chart"), *and they deliver them.*

Further, if you meet an attractive person in an Enneagram or numerology class, the free flow of second-chakra energy between you will not be inhibited by the anti-erotic constrictions of the therapeutic milieu. You can go home with your "hot number" without processing the experience to death—and without worrying that you'll miss anything by leaving class early. You already have the most important piece of information: you're a perfect ten, and you know it.

HOW TO MEET THE CHALLENGE

1. Find a Metaphysician Who Makes House Calls

New Age self-help jargon makes fine fodder at cocktail parties and Pilates classes, but such airheaded delusions as "trusting in the universe" and "believing that things happen for a reason" are not the Narcissist Way. We know whom and what we can place our trust in: no one and nothing. We know why things happen: because we make them happen. *That* is the Narcissist Way, and *that* must be the guiding light of our descent into the mystic.

First Ladies, rock stars, and *New York Times* best-selling authors have their own astrologers, tarot card readers, cosmologists, *and* cosmetologists on staff—as every narcissist should. When interviewing candidates for your personal metaphysician, check the diplomas on his/her office (or yurt or geodesic dome) wall; make sure they were issued by a prestigious institution. You don't want to end up with a metaphysician who cheated on his metaphysics exams by looking into the soul of the student next to him.

2. Roll Your Own

If you failed to absorb the lessons of Step Three: Marriage and/or Step Five: Career, and therefore cannot afford to retain the services of an on-staff metaphysician, you need not resign yourself to the unimaginative metaphysical tools used by OPGs (Ordinary Personal Growers). Instead, purchase your own contemporary, top-quality, narcissist-appropriate Transcendental Toolkit.

> **The *Enough About You*™ Do-It-Yourself-Help Transcendental Toolkit contains everything the narcissist needs to conduct his/her own metaphysical therapy. Now offered at the special price of $74.95, this validating value-pack includes:**
>
> - One-eighth of an ounce of sommelier-selected, smoky yet voluptuous Wuyi Oolong tea leaves, for suitably sophisticated readings
>
> - The "Deposed CEO" Tarot deck, featuring likenesses of narcissist executives we have known, loved, and imprisoned
>
> - The Self-Lover's Astrology Chart, highlighting the signs most favorable to narcissists, including: "70% Off," "Valet Parking," "Do Not Disturb," "Rodeo Drive," and "Invited Guests Only."
>
> - The *Enough About You*™ limited edition "Me-Ching"
>
> **AVAILABLE OPTION: Purchase the Overextended MimiCare Protection Plan for just $249/year, and you won't need a crystal ball to guarantee the emotional, psychic, and technical support of**

our skilled, empathetic *Enough About You*™ Technical Occultants. Whatever your problem, no need to talk about it: they'll sense it before you say it.

3. When You Wish Upon a Star . . .

. . . you're likely to achieve about the same results as those you'll attain using any of the self-improvement methods described above. This confirms what numerous scientific studies, as well as thousands of disgruntled, personal growth–stunted customers, have found: there is little if any difference between the outcomes of therapy clients, workshop participants, and metaphysical seekers versus those who use more commonplace, "home-grown" techniques.

So if those "human speed bumps"—the people with the unfortunate power to impinge upon the perfect life you deserve—are still insisting that you "become a better person," try getting what you (they) want the old-fashioned way. Find a four-leaf clover. Carry a (Bulgari faux-fur) rabbit's foot. Blow out the candles on your (three-tiered, twenty-four-candled, 94 percent cacao Belgian chocolate) birthday cake. Or just do what narcissists throughout history have done so often and so well: fake it.

Putting the "Me" Back in Memoir

If every age has its disorder—hysteria in Freud's Vienna, addiction in the eighties, depression in the nineties—ours seems to be the age of narcissism.

—*VOGUE*, OCTOBER 2002

What do they mean, "disorder"?

—MIMI E. GOTIST, OCTOBER 2002

When Ordinary Authors write books, the process is an utterly unempowering one, from grueling start to anticlimactic finish. OAs spend years in their dismal little Ikea-furnished rooms, researching, writing, rewriting, only to have their editors misinterpret them, their publicists underpromote them, their reviewers ravage them, and their audiences abandon them. When their books are published, OAs bitterly file their red-ink-laden royalty statements in their oak veneer desks, assemble their reviews (all bad, and so few of them) into tacky cardboard scrapbooks, gulp down a bottle or two of bottom-shelf scotch, shake their incompetently coiffed heads, and start to work on yet another soon-to-be-worst-selling tome.

Pas moi. As a Narcissist Author and member of BLAABLAA (Bibliophiles' Latent Activist Band of Literary American Assertives), I am proud to say that I have retained creative control of this book, every Manolo Blahnik–shod step of the way.

For the accomplishment of this literary coup, I have no one to thank but myself. It was I who insisted on hourly consultations (more, as needed) with my editor, and daily meetings with the editor-in-chief. It was I who lured Madonna's publicist from the now-immaterial Material Girl and hired him as my own. (Shhh! My publisher doesn't know it yet, but it will be *he* who pays the bill!) It was I who researched the favorite flowers, preferred truffle flavors, and dirty little secrets of every book reviewer, talk show host, and chain bookstore CEO in the nation—and I who made such good use of my findings.

Thanks to my efforts—and yours now, dear reader—I am confident that this book will find its way into the hands of those who await its imminent arrival with bated breath, professionally bleached teeth, and disposable income at the ready. It is my fondest hope that my loyal fans—you, dear reader—will purchase this book and its many "me-quels" in record-breaking numbers, and that the benefits you realize will justify the days—*weeks* actually—of hard work that went into it.

I share these behind-the-scenes autobiographical details with you now not to brag (although I would be well within my rights to do so), but as a generously instructive case in point. Just as an assertive, self-empowered, self-loving Narcissist Author such as myself can "write her own story," allowing no one and nothing to sabotage her meteoric ascent to the apex of literary success, so can narcissists of all stripes (vertical only, please!) hydroplane above the rough seas of fate, skimming over the churning currents in which so many Ordinary Persons flail, sink, and drown, earning the two-word review every Narcissist Author dreams of: "Millions Sold."

If all that self-help hype they swallow the way I myself imbibe Mimitinis (three ounces iced Grey Goose vodka, six citrus-stuffed olives on the side) were truly of any "help" at all, OPs would have the self-esteem it takes to aspire to narcissism, instead of resorting to disparaging it. If all those personal growth workshops they attend as often as I myself visit my colorist yielded the promised "growth," OPs would be "big" enough to imitate, not scorn, the biggest people who walk the earth today. But then, they wouldn't be OPs if they could visualize something better for themselves: something more like, well, *us*.

In a world dominated by Ordinary Persons, narcissists are blamed for everything from terrorism to the "character flaws" of our society's most interesting, successful, *self-assured* people and corporations: "overpaid" athletes, "difficult" actors, "arrogant" lifestyle magnates, "promiscuous" presidents, "ruthless" CEOs, "obnoxious" cocktail party guests. The cause of this demonization is as crystal-clear as a freshly shaken Mimitini. Because OPs cannot emulate us, they envy us. Because they cannot navigate the pinnacles of our path, they pathologize us. Lacking the wherewithal to be like us, they belittle, besmirch, and berate us. Try as they might to reduce us to smaller, more "manageable" versions of the larger-than-life personalities we are, ultimately every OP must face this truth: you can lead a narcissist to mediocrity, but you can't make him shrink.

And so I say to my detractors, as all narcissists must say to theirs: clicks and roam will break up my phone, but nerds will never harm me. If my words of wisdom offend or enrage you, I offer no apology, but this suggestion instead: make use of the one self-help tool that has worked so well for me, and narcissists everywhere, since our namesake first glanced into that pond. Look into that mirror. Look hard. Look long. Look deep.

And if the Blahnik fits—wear it.

Begrudging Acknowledgments

What a travesty: being forced to "acknowledge" the Ordinary People who sat idly by, waiting to cash in on my creativity, while I slaved to produce the compendium of wit and wisdom that is *Enough About You*.

My editor argues (pointing menacingly to the line in my contract that stipulates "payment on delivery of an acceptable manuscript") that writing "generous" acknowledgments will make me appear more human (as if *that's* something to which I would aspire). Now I understand why every Ordinary Author's book ends with simpering, self-effacing praise for everyone on earth except the one person who deserves it: the author him/herself. As, alas, will mine. Herewith, I do what must be done.

In writing this book, I cleverly assembled a team whose expertise and devotion surpassed even my exacting standards: my funnier-than-he-thinks-he-is, smarter-than-anyone-other-than-Mimi-has-a-right-to-be editor, Gideon Weil; the incisively insightful and delightfully dedicated Anne Connolly; Calla Devlin, publicist *sans pareil;* my terrifyingly simpatico designer/illustrator, Kris Tobiassen, my inspiringly indefatigable literary agent, Amy Rennert; and my appropriately adoring (and fortunately, forgiving) bride, Catherine Thomas-Gotist.

A big Mimi kiss-kiss to Suzy Parker, Lonny Shavelson, Maggie Estep, and Patricia McCormick for the well-deserved and unbridled enthusiasm they continue to manifest for this project and, well, for me.

And a special thank-you to Lynn Gordon, whether she wants it or not.

About the Type

This book was set in Narcissus Boldfacias, a well-proportioned, unnecessarily humble typeface first designed for the writings of Nero in the first century A.D. Narcissus Boldfacias was brought to the New World by Christopher Columbus in the midfifteenth century. It has since been adapted for modern usage, most notably by an anonymous vocalist—a well-known connoisseur of the beautiful face—who has commissioned a world-renowned linotypographer to have the words to every Beatles song typeset in this adaptable yet elegant font.

About Mimi

Mimi E. Gotist is the *nom de plume* of an incredibly gifted, dead-serious, best-selling author. She hopes (and deserves) to divide her time between Hollywood, various Ritz-Carltons, and her cosmetic surgeon's office.

Contact Mimi

Mimi adores fan mail. Please contribute generously to the cause.

via the internet:
www.mimiegotist.com

or the quaint yet enduring way:
Mimi E. Gotist
c/o HarperSanFrancisco
353 Sacramento Street, Suite 500
San Francisco, California 94111

Please be advised, however, that the author's *Enough About You*™ Personal Data Organizer will sort incoming messages, giving top priority to those containing offers that are both lucrative and gratifying.